FOURTH EDITION

SMALL HOTELS & INNS OF ANDALUCÍA

CHARMING PLACES TO STAY IN SOUTHERN SPAIN

Guy Hunter-Watts

SANTANA BOOKS

SMALL HOTELS & INNS OF ANDALUCÍA (4th Edition)

Published by Ediciones Santana, S.L.
Apartado 41
29650 Mijas-Pueblo (Málaga)
Spain

Tel: (0034) 952 48 58 38
Fax: (0034) 952 48 53 67
E-Mail: info@santanabooks.com
Website: www.santanabooks.com

First published in September 2001
Second edition: February 2004
Third edition: April 2006
Fourth edition: April 2008

Designed by New Image Communications, S.L.

Printed in Spain by Gráficas San Pancracio, S.L.

ISBN: 978-84-89954-75-5
Depósito Legal: MA-565/2008

This book is dedicated to Tikizani, with love and thanks...

ABOUT THE AUTHOR

Guy Hunter-Watts first came to Andalucía in the early eighties when he cycled across the country on an old push bike. It was a life-changing journey. He was so taken by Spain and its people that he returned to the UK and enrolled at university in Bristol to study Spanish language and culture.

After graduation he travelled to South America where he taught at a university in Colombia and then, inspired by the magic of the Andes, led tours there for many years. India and Mongolia came next and after several years of semi-nomadic life he set up home in the mountains west of Ronda.

His wanderlust has been satiated, in part, by visiting hundreds of small hotels and B&Bs throughout France, Spain, South Africa and Morocco.

Guy is also author of Santana's *Walking in Andalucía*, a guide to some of the best walks in southern Spain's National Parks.

ACKNOWLEDGEMENTS

This book owes its existence, in large part, to Alastair Sawday. It was thanks to him that I first started beating about Europe visiting hotels and B&Bs for his 'Special Places to Stay' series. His books have set new standards and Alastair has been tireless in his efforts to promote small hotels with a human face. He has helped to get ethics back on the travel agenda and his books are part of his long battle against corporate monoculture. This book, like his own series, is inspired in the belief that 'Small is Beautiful' and that we are all in need of places to stay with a more human face.

As a freelance journalist I have got to know about a number of new places thanks to my work for www.i-escape.com. So thanks to Nikki Tinto, Nadine Mellor and Mike Cullen for sending me off to stay in some delectable hotels which are included for the first time within these pages.

As always, friends and readers have let me know about their own discoveries. Mike Lewin has been heading off into the Andalucían hinterland for the best part of four decades, digging out interesting places to stay for location crews as well as for himself and his family. As always, thanks to you too, Mike, for sharing your recommendations.

And to Cheryl Gatward of New Image Communications a big thank you, too, for all of your hard work and creativity when it came to the design and layout of this latest edition of the book.

My gratitude is also due to readers of this guide who have written to me about their experiences when staying at listings in this book. This feedback was invaluable when it came to deciding which places should be included in this present edition and, in just a few cases, which places were no longer worthy of an entry.

And a final ¡gracias! to the owners and staff of the places included in this book who welcome us all with good grace and generosity. Without you all, travelling in Andalucía wouldn't be nearly as much fun.

CONTENTS

CONTENTS

An analogy might be made between the Andalucían small hotel scene and its wines. In the decade following the Seville Expo, riding the Brussels gravy train, a plethora of small hotels were born. Like young *mosto* wine they had a lot of attitude and it was good to have them around. But occasionally you were left wanting something...well, a little smoother. Most of them were conceived in a distinctly rustic vein: this was, after all, the prevailing fashion of the time. It seemed that hoteliers thought that so long as they had a few beams and terracotta tiles it was enough to make an inn or hotel a success.

But things soon began to bed down and improve and it was the visitors themselves who were the biggest motor for change. Northen Europeans wanted more for breakfast than coffee and cup cakes, or juice from a carton. They were taller and needed bigger beds, others were more demanding when it came to warm rooms, big towels and decent tea, and the clamour for more interesting salads and vegetarian food was growing. Well-heeled *sevillanos* and *gaditanos* who were out-on-the-weekend – rural tourism was getting fashionable amongst the Spanish, too – weren't afraid to pay the double for a decent plate of *ibérico* rather than *serrano* ham, nor for a decent bottle of wine.

Change was in the air and restaurants and hotels were obliged to sink or swim. And by the time we saw in the New Millenium things were changing apace. It was as if instead of *mosto* we were now being treated to a good *Rioja* or *Ribera del Duero*, to something that you knew would be consistently enjoyable. The whole movement reached critical mass then began to gather momentum.

Whilst standards of accommodation were getting better and better, the food scene also began to improve. That isn't to say that there hasn't always been good food in Andalucía: I'd never knock its country cuisine and we all know just how good a *potaje de lentejas*, some good *rabo de toro* or *conejo al ajillo* can be. But as well as these time-tried recipes more innovative food was now being magicked up by a new generation of young chefs. Fusion had become the buzz word and food became more cosmopolitan. The debt to the flavours of the Maghreb was celebrated rather than denied.

Within these pages you'll find a spicier selection of hotels than was the case with the third edition. Andalucía continues its historical metamorphosis: this is an area of Europe that has always seemed at ease with assimilating cultures different to its own.

We now stand, or so it would seem, at a crossroads. As well those delightful rustic village inns the 'boutique' hotel has made its *entrée en scène* in Andalucía with a big splash. When researching this guide it was fascinating to discover that in Sevilla, Cádiz, Málaga and Granada small hotels have all opened which model themselves on the *riads* of Morocco, those chic converted townhouses which have sprung up in great numbers in Marrakech and Fes. In the same way that restauranteurs are opening up to new culinary trends, hoteliers are looking further afield for inspiration. To stay in some of these design hotels is an expensive treat but you may agree that they are worth the extra euros. And again, the wine analogy seems to hold: where once people were content with a wine from La Rioja they now search out a *vino de autor,* an individual blend of grapes that varies from each special bottle to special bottle.

So within these pages you'll find a spicier, more varied selection of hotels than was the case with the third edition. Andalucía continues its historical metamorphosis: this is an area of Europe that has always seemed at ease with assimilating cultures different to its own. In the case of the Moors it was a long, slow process, taking place over several centuries. In this Brave New World of the Internet and multiculturalism the latest influences are being felt much more quickly. Whilst embracing the positive sides of a more mobile, interconnected world we should be quick to defend the deeper-rooted culture of Andalucía that makes travel here so rewarding.

OUR CRITERIA FOR INCLUDING PLACES &
WHAT MAKES THIS BOOK DIFFERENT TO OTHER HOTEL GUIDES

When researching this guide I visited many more places than those that were eventually included. The fact that some failed to make it into these pages is no reflection on their professionalism. They were simply places that I might not stay at given other choices in the area. This is bound to be a subjective decision but I hope that I've developed an idea of what might appeal to most readers.

You'll find hotels and B&Bs for all tastes and all budgets within the pages of this book. The bottom line for including a particular hotel or B&B is that it must be clean, friendly, comfortable as well as exceptional in one way or another. Just what constitutes 'exceptional' can vary enormously: it might be the building itself, the views from the terrace, the peacefulness (always high on my personal check list) or the proximity to, say, the Mezquita in Córdoba or the Alhambra in Granada. Every single place listed here has a location that is special in some way.

Inevitably, in certain areas, I've included more places to stay than in others. This is the case of Vejer de la Frontera where in the last couple of years half a dozen really great places have been opened. The same holds true for Ronda and its surrounding *sierras*. The fact that there are several listings reflects a simple fact of travelling life: many more people visit these areas. I've also included half a dozen more expensive city listings in this edition of the guide. Personally I'd think twice before spending, say, €250 on a bed for the night. But we all have those events to celebrate and these hotels might be the place for a splurge.

If you read the text carefully for any given listing and you should be able to garner why I like it and of any misgivings that I might have. There is, after all, no such thing as hotel perfection. So be tolerant of a hotel's eccentricities and individuality: you'll find no chain hotel uniformity within these pages.

Finally I should point out two unusual things about this guide.

The first is that I personally visited each and every one of the places listed for THIS edition of the book. This means that this book is bound to be more reliable

than others that simply send out a questionnaire asking for revised price lists. It was a huge amount of work but means that I really can put my hand on my heart and say 'I know these places pretty well'.

Secondly, and most importantly, NO HOTEL PAYS TO BE INCLUDED IN THIS GUIDE. A number of hotels agreed to buy a few books from us but it wasn't a pre-condition for entry. What this means for you, the reader, is that you have in your hands 'la crème de la crème' of what Andalucía has to offer.

Owners/staff **speak English**

 Hotel has room(s) with **full disabled facilities** (see 1)

 Bedrooms have **air-conditioning**

 Hotel has its **own swimming pool**

 Pets are accepted, regardless of size (see 2)

 Vegetarian food can be prepared (see 3)

 Credit Cards are accepted

 Good walks close to the hotel

 Garden/patio area where guests can sit outside

 Hotel is suitable/caters for **young children** (see 4)

 Hotel has its **own car park** (see 5)

 Invitation to **welcome drink** if you show this guide

 Hotel has either wifi **Internet connection** or computer for guests to use

NOTES

1. Always check on exact facilities if you have any disabilities

2. House rules can vary. Some hotels allow dogs in rooms, other only in purpose-built kennels. Always check.

3. If you have special dietary requirements let the hotel know prior to your arrival.

4. Check before you arrive what is available in the way of cots, baby-sitter, etc.

5. Some city-centre hotel car parks aren't adjacent to the hotel: check before you arrive.

PAGE NUMBERS

The hotels are grouped by provinces - there are 8 in Andalucía - and have been numbered on a west to east basis, beginning with Huelva and ending with Almería. The flagged number on the map corresponds to the actual page number of the hotel.

You'll find the number of the map on which any hotel is flagged indicated on its page in the book.

INDEXES

At the back of this book you'll find hotels indexed both by name and by location. When searching out any particular place the first letter of the complete title is used to place it in the index. So, for example, Hotel Zuhayara is listed under 'H' and La Cazalla under 'L'.

ADDRESSES

Occasionally the address which appears in the book is a hotel's postal address and not that of the hotel itself. When you come to visiting a place simply follow instructions in the 'directions' section and you should have no problem in finding it.

WEB PAGES/EMAIL

A hotel's web site can, of course, give you a great deal more information than we can in this guide and is always worth a quick visit, especially if you are planning a stay of several nights. Many websites now give you the exact coordinates of a hotel's location. This can be useful although I do still find that hotel owners and their staff can guide you more quickly to your hotel than an in-car navigation system.

DESCRIPTION

Remember that this is my personal reaction to /assessment of a place and it might differ in some way to yours. Please let me know (email me at info@rondatejar.com) if you disagree with anything or if you think that something is missing from the description.

WELCOME DRINK

All of the places with the 'welcome drink' symbol will happily offer you a drink on arrival if you show them a copy of your Santana guide. Many, it must be said, do this as a matter of course.

ROOMS

I've tried to make it clear what the exact bed configuration is of any hotel. Occasionally hotels differ over what they describe as a suite. Some see it as a large bedroom with enough space for a couple of easy chairs and/or a sofa (also sometimes referred to as 'junior' suite) whilst for others the term is only used if there is a completely separate lounge. If the latter is important to you then check at the time of booking.

PRICES

The prices quoted for rooms and food are those of 2008. If you are using this book after then, be prepared for a small increase. But it would be unusual for these to have gone up by more than 10%. Again, check on web page at the time of booking.

MEALS

Breakfast: Anyone who has lived in Spain for any length of time will know that breakfast here can be a rather meagre affair. Things are improving but in many hotels the standard offering is simply toast and jam with coffee or tea. Fresh orange juice is becoming more common but don't automatically expect it. Be aware, too, that breakfast often doesn't get going in some places until 9am. If you need to get on the road before then, you'd be best to pay your bill the night before. At some city hotels I tend to skip the included buffet and slip out and take in a bit of street life at a local cafe.

Lunch/Dinner: The price that we have quoted in the book for meals is generally that of the set menu or, occasionally when there is not one available, the average price that you'd expect to pay for a three course meal. Be aware that waiters often don't automatically tell you what's available on the set menu so always ask (¿hay menú del día?). This can often be the best thing to eat because the chances are that it will have been slow-cooked and prepared on the same day. Dining à la carte can often be two or three times more expensive than the set meal.

We have included the dates/days of the week when some places close their restaurants. But always check when booking that food will be available. In many of the smaller places included here it is essential to let your hosts know if you would like to eat supper on the evening of your arrival.

DIRECTIONS

Again, I hope, largely self-explanatory.

The space that we have for describing how to find any given place is limited. Many hotels will happily email more detailed route notes/maps for finding them. And many have detailed instructions on their web pages as well as exact GPS coordinates.

The Michelin map of Andalucía, no. 446, is pretty good and takes account of the recent renumbering of many of our roads.

STAR RATINGS

I don't list these in this book and don't set much store by them. There are five star hotels that have as much character as your average potting shed and one star hotels which are fit for a King.

Did you know that to get that fabled fifth star you need, amongst other things, three phones in each bedroom? I can happily manage with one or none. And how do you give a smile a star rating?

So I resolutely ignored star ratings when researching this book.

GENERAL INFORMATION & PRACTICALITIES

REGISTRATION

Spanish law still requires you to register on arrival at any hotel in Spain and you will need to produce your passport/I.D.. This can seem like an ordeal when you arrive after a long drive but remember that this is as tedious for hotel staff as it is for you. Once a hotel's staff have noted down the details of your passport, however, they have no right to keep hold of it. I personally always retrieve my passport immediately so as to avoid forgetting it the next day.

LANGUAGE

Many travellers in Andalucía express amazement when they come across hotel reception and restaurant staff who speak virtually no English. Be tolerant of this and remember that few hotel workers in our home countries would be able to converse easily in Spanish. People try hard but they have often not had the benefit of learning a foreign language at school.

Remember, too, that a few words of Spanish, even of the pidgin variety, can go a long way.

CHILDREN

Nearly all hotels in Andalucía welcome children and find it amazing that there are places that don't. If you're travelling with very young children it's best to ring ahead and ask exactly which facilities are available: don't automatically assume that there will be cots and high chairs. Occasionally hotels can organise baby-sitting ('servicio de kangúru') but should be given advance warning.

BOOKING / CREDIT CARDS

Be aware that it is quite normal for hotels to ask for a credit card number when you make a reservation by phone or by Email. The standard practice is to charge the cost of the first night against your card. This is generally a non-refundable deposit. According to Spanish law a hotel shouldn't debit your card for more than the cost of one night for every ten booked.

Some people are wary of giving card details over the phone. But you should know that, to date, I've never heard of a case of fraud and that many hotels operate in this way because of the number of no-shows, particularly common with weekend tourism. When the weather turns bad that trip to the country can suddenly seem a whole lot less attractive.

Remember, too, that a few of the smaller, B&B-type places in this guide don't accept payment by credit card. We include a symbol to let you know those which do take plastic. And you will rarely be far away from a cash dispenser.

ARRIVAL / DEPARTURE TIMES

Some hotels have a policy of holding rooms (with or without a credit card details) until early evening - normally about 20h - then letting the room if you haven't shown up. If you're running late be sure to give a quick call to let the hotel know that you are still coming.

And remember that in Spain, as in other countries, most places require you to vacate your room by 12h. If you want to leave later, however, most hotels will be happy to look after your luggage.

HEATING

Most of Andalucía's hotels have been designed primarily with keeping cool in mind. Anybody who has lived for long in southern Spain will know that winters can be wet and cold. If you're headed for one of the more simple places included here it is always worth reminding the hotel of your estimated time of arrival and requesting that radiators are turned on before you get there. In addition remember that those same marble floors, which are so pleasant in summer, can be an ordeal in winter. So pack a pair of thick socks or slippers!

NOISE

You may not be aware that the Spanish ear is subject to a higher decibel onslaught than any other ear in Europe. Anyone living in Spain will be aware of the Spaniards' love of getting together in large groups and eating and drinking into the early hours. Hotels are, by nature, places where you're likely to come across people who are in party mode and two o'clock in the morning is still early by Friday / Saturday night standards.

If you're a light sleeper ask for a quiet room at the time of booking and be aware that some of the grander 'cortijo' style places are often used for wedding parties at weekends.

And if you're given a noisy room don't feel awkward about asking to be moved.

NAVIGATING IN THE CITY CENTRES

Córdoba, Granada and Sevilla and some of the larger towns in Andalucía like Arcos de la Frontera and Ronda can be tricky places to negotiate when it comes to finding your hotel even if you have GPS in-car navigation. Seeing that nearly all hotels charge around €15-20 for using their car park it can save you a huge amount of hassle to simply leave your car at any city centre car park then take a taxi to your hotel.

If the amount of baggage you have with you makes this awkward it might be advisable to stop a taxi and ask the driver to lead you to your hotel. It can save you masses of time, and heartache, and it would be rare to clock up more than €10 in fares.

YOUR OPINION/RECOMMENDATIONS

You may have your own favourite hotel that doesn't appear in this guide. Please let me know about places which you think deserve to be included and also if you feel that any of my listings haven't matched up to your expectations. With your feedback this guide will improve with each subsequent edition.

I'd especially welcome your comments about your gastronomic experiences. When I visit any hotel I can only sample one or two dishes and so it can be difficult to get the 'big picture'. Please let me know of any particular hits (or misses) and also of any wines that you've really enjoyed.

Please email me your comments to info@rondatejar.com

Many thanks.

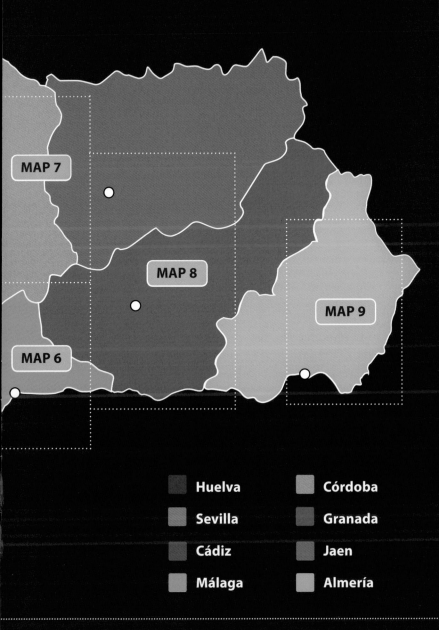

MAP 7

MAP 8

MAP 9

MAP 6

- Huelva
- Sevilla
- Cádiz
- Málaga
- Córdoba
- Granada
- Jaen
- Almería

MAP 1

1 Encinasola

Cumbres Mayores

Arroyomolinos de León

La Nava

Hinojales

2

Jabugo

6

Cala

Aroche

Cortegana

Aracena

Higuera de la Sierra

3

4 **5**

Zufre

Sᵗᵃ Bárbara de Casa

San Telmo

Campofrío

Valdelamusa

Cabezas Rubias

Tharsis

Zalamea La Real

Villanueva de las Cruces

Berrocal

Alosno

Valverde del Camino

San Bartolomé de la Torre

Beas

Manzanilla

Gibraleón

Niebla

Trigueros

Chucena

Rociana del Condado

Hinojos

Aljaraque

Bonares

Cartaya

HUELVA

Moguer

Almonte

Palos de la Frontera

8

Punta Umbría

El Rocio

7

Matalascañas

MAP 2

Alanis

14

Las Navas de la
Concepción

Cazalla
de la Sierra

15

El Pedroso

Constantina

Castilblanco
de los Arroyos

Lora del Río

Villanueva del Río

Burguillos

Tocina

Guillena

Brenes

La Campana

Gerena

Alcalá del Río

Aznalcollar

La Rinconada

Carmona

La Algaba

Olivares

13   **12** ✈

16

Camas

Huevar

11   SEVILLA

Mairena
del Alcor

Tomares

Benacazón

10

Aznalcazar

9

Alcalá de Guadaira

Marchena

Coria
del Río

Dos
Hermanas

Paradas

Los Palacios
y Villafranca

Utrera

Arahal

Los Molares

Vilafranco del
Guadalquivir

Morón
de la Frontera

Palmar
de Troya

El Coronil

19

Las Cabezas
de San Juan

20

Montellano

Lebrija

MAP 3

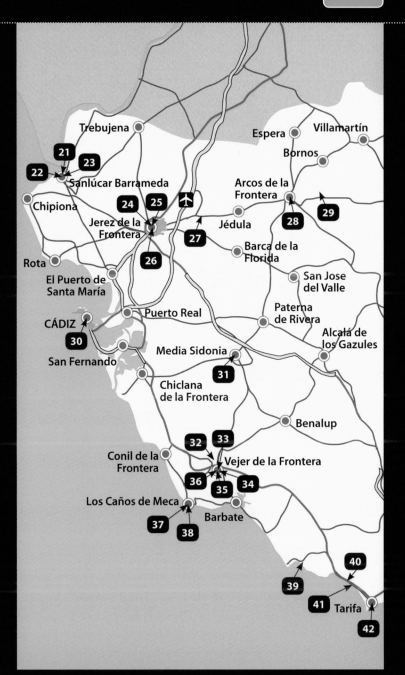

MAP 4

Trebujena

Espera   Villamartín

Bornos

21

23

22

Sanlúcar Barrameda

Chipiona

Arcos de la
Frontera

24   25   ✈

29

Jerez de la
Frontera

Jédula

28

27

26

Barca de la
Florida

Rota

San Jose
del Valle

El Puerto de
Santa María

Puerto Real

Paterna
de Rivera

CÁDIZ

30

Alcalá de
los Gazules

San Fernando

Media Sidonia

31

Chiclana
de la Frontera

Benalup

32   33

Conil de la
Frontera

Vejer de la Frontera

36   34

35

Los Caños de Meca

Barbate

37

38

40

39

41   Tarifa

42

MAP 5

Campillos

Almargen

Teba

Cañete La Real

Algondonales

59

57

60

62

63

Cuevas
del Becerro

Ardales

El Burgo

47

Grazalema

58

61

64

66

Ronda

65

Yunqera

Alozaina

56

55

Tolox

69

Alozaina

Ubrique

Cortes de la
Frontera

67

68

70

72

Guaro

Istán

75

Ojén

54

52

53

Benahavís

73

49

Guacín

51

71

74

Marbella

46

50

San Pedro
de Alcántara

Jimena de
la Frontera

45

Casares

48

Estepona

San Martín
de Tessorillo

Manilva

43

Castellar de
la Frontera

44

San Roque

Algeciras

Gibraltar

MAP 6

Cuevas de San Marco
Alameda
Mollina
Sierra de Yeguas
Villanueva de Algaidas
90
Campillos
Humilladero
Archidona
Antequera
85
Villanueva del Rosario
Villanueva de la Concepción
80
84
82
Ríogordo
Periana
Ardales
81
Casabermeja
Colmenar
92
Casarabonela
Alora
86
Vélez Málaga
83
Almogia
91
Pizarra
Benamocarra
Alozaina
87
Guaro
Cártama
Alhaurin el Grande
89
MÁLAGA
93
Coín
76
88
Rincón de la Victoria
75
Ojén
Torremolinos
Mijas
77
Benalmádena
74
79
73
Marbella
Fuengirola
78

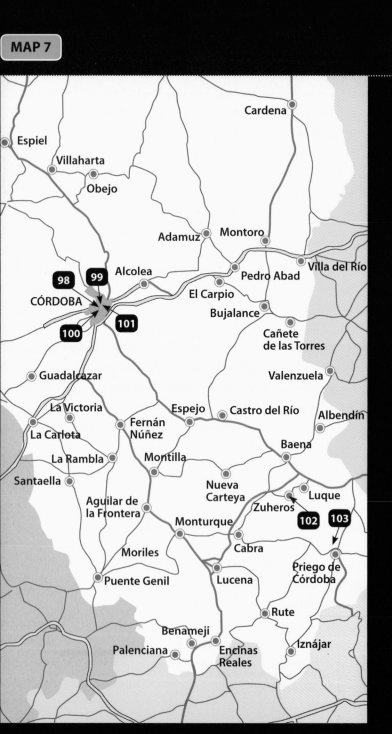

MAP 7

Cardena

Espiel

Villaharta

Obejo

Adamuz • Montoro

Villa del Río

Alcolea • Pedro Abad

98 **99**

CÓRDOBA

El Carpio

Bujalance

100 **101**

Cañete
de las Torres

Guadalcazar

Valenzuela

La Victoria

Espejo • Castro del Río • Albendín

Fernán
Núñez

La Carlota

Baena

La Rambla • Montilla

Santaella

Nueva
Carteya • Luque

Aguilar de
la Frontera • Zuheros

102 **103**

Monturque

Moriles • Cabra

Puente Genil • Lucena

Priego de
Córdoba

Rute

Benameji

Palenciana • Encinas
Reales • Iznájar

Bailén

Linares

N-322 **123**

Santo Tomé

Baeza Úbeda **124**

122 Cazorla

Peal de Becerro

Fuerte del Rey

Jimena Jódar Quesada **125**

A-316 JAÉN

Martos Mancha Real Huesa

Los Villares Cambil

Carchalejo Huelma

Castillo de Locubin

Domingo Perez

Alcalá La Real Campotéjar Pedro Martínez

Pinar Fonelas

Colomera

Puerto López Darro Guadix

104 Pinos

Montefrío Puente

GRANADA La Peza

105 Tocón **111** **112** Lugros

Chimeneas **110** Quentar

113

Mala **109**

106 **114**

Agron N-323 **118**

108 Trevélez **119** Laroles

Alhama de **115** Valor

Granada Jayena Cadiar **121**

94 Albuñuelas Lanjarón **120**

95 Órgiva **117**

96 Otivar **116** Albunol

Torrox N-340

Nerja Motril

97 Alumñécar

107

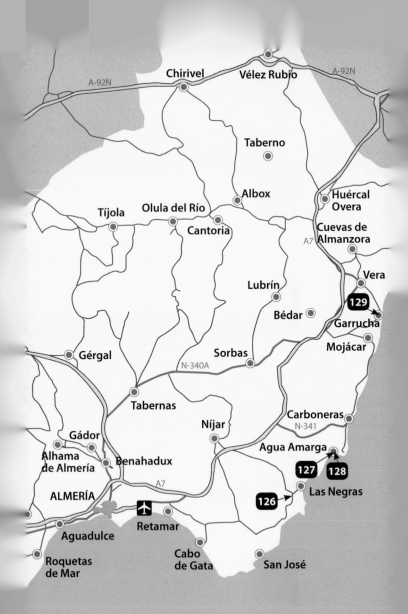

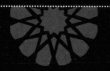

HOTELS 001 – 008

HUELVA

HOTEL RINCÓN DEL ABADE

Llano de San Juan s/n, 21390 Encinasola

Tel: 959 714 536 Fax: 959 714 327

Email: informacion@rincondelabade.com

www.rincondelabade.com

Management:	Ana María Pérez Ríos
Closed:	Never
Bedrooms:	1 Single, 17 Doubles and 3 Suites
Prices:	Single €27, Double €50, Suite €50 + 7% VAT
Meals:	Breakfast €2-5, Lunch/Dinner approx. €20

Directions: From Aracena take N433 towards Portugal then N345 towards Badajóz. On reaching Higuera la Real turn left to Encinasola. Hotel on left as you arrive in village.

The name Encinasola probably won't ring many inner bells. This tiny village is hidden away in the most northwesterly corner of Huelva province and gets little in the way of passing traffic. Yet it is surrounded by a lovely sweep of rolling *dehesa*, the walking is fabulous and you are well placed for day trips to Portugal which is just a few miles distant. Arriving from the east you'll have no problem spotting the hotel, a solid edifice of dressed stone at the edge of the village. As soon as you step inside the place wraps you in a warm embrace: wafer bricks, beamed and planked ceilings, terracotta tiles and fine stonework have been beautifully crafted to create the ambience of a traditional *onubense* house. Ana, Abade's young manager, greets you with a natural spontaneity of the type that can't be learned in any school of tourism. When she shows you your room you may be tempted to question the price. Can it really be so little? The best bedrooms are those which are tucked up beneath the eaves. They have every creature comfort, first class mattresses and even though some of the prints and other memorabilia are a tad sugary, they are quiet, spotless and cosy. And downstairs is a pretty restaurant whose menu sticks to traditional mountain fare and next door a lively bar where you'll soon strike up conversation with the locals. *Reductions on room prices for longer stays!*

To see & do nearby: Walking in the Aracena mountains, day trips to Portugal and to Zafra, Jerez de los Caballeros and Almendralejo.

FINCA LA SILLADILLA

21290 Los Romeros/Jabugo

Tel: 959 501 350 or 647 913 167 Fax: 959 501 351

Email: silladi@teleline.es

www.jabugo.cc

Management:	Maia Araujo
Closed:	Never
Bedrooms:	1 Twin, 1 Suite, 3 Houses with 2 bedrooms and 1 House with 3 bedrooms
Prices:	Twin €76-89, Suite €89-108, 2 bedroomed House €152-172, 3 bedroomed House €228-267 including VAT and cleaning
Meals:	Breakfast included, no other meals apart from snacks: buy ingredients from farm shop

Directions: From Sevilla A66/E803 north towards Mérida then N433 towards Portugal. Bypass Aracena, then Jabugo, and just past El Repilado turn left towards Los Romeros. After 3 kms turn left at sign for La Silladilla.

You may well have heard of Jabugo ham, that mouth-watering delicacy that has always been a favourite present to diplomats visiting Spain, adding a certain weight to that farewell handshake at Madrid's Barajas airport. But the chances are you won't have heard of Finca La Silladilla which is hidden away in a sea of cistus and oak-forest in a little-known corner of Huelva. You journey here by way of winding country lanes and a narrow stonewalled track which leads up to the farm – a sight for the sorest of travel-weary eyes. Your room will either be in the main farmhouse or in one of two nearby cottages. The decoration and furnishings are stylish but not in the least showy; a nice mix of bright fabrics and local base elements like granite, terracotta and chestnut wood. Although Silladilla's young live-in staff serve only breakfast (outside in summer, in your room when temperatures fall), there's a bar doubling as a shop/delicatessen where you can buy the makings of a gourmet supper - including, of course, the best Jabugo ham. Wine enthusiasts will appreciate the carefully selected bottles and the prices, too. If you prefer to dine out you're a hop away from some of Sierra's prettiest villages and there are some fabulous walks in the area (see my book *Walking in Andalucía*).

To see & do nearby: Visit to one of the Jabugo ham *secaderos* (drying sheds), walking in the Natural Park of Aracena, trips to Portugal.

CASA GARCÍA

Avenida de San Martín 2, 21350 Almonaster la Real

Tel: 959 143 109 Fax: 959 143 233
Email: casagarcia@ozu.es
www.hotelcasagarcia.com

Management:	Juan García Portero
Closed:	Never
Bedrooms:	3 Doubles, 18 Twins and 1 Suite
Prices:	Double/Twin €50, Suite €91 + 7% VAT
Meals:	Breakfast €6, Lunch/Dinner €15-20 excluding wine

Directions: From Aracena take the N433 towards Portugal. Shortly before reaching Cortegana turn left to Almonaster. Casa García is on the right at the entrance to the village.

Almonaster la Real is one of the loveliest of a string of mountain villages which stretch west through the Aracena Park towards the Portuguese border. When out walking the ancient footpaths which link the villages I felt as if I were rediscovering the Wessex described by Hardy. The García family have been feeding locals for almost three decades but it was only recently that they revamped a simple village eatery to create a stylish and comfortable small hotel-cum-restaurant. You arrive by way of a shady terrace, a great place from where to watch the world (and the occasional car or donkey) pass you by. On the two floors above are the bedrooms whose comfort and quality will take you by surprise given their paltry price tag. The floor plan of some is slightly puzzling - some rooms are rather long and narrow - but they work well enough. Forego a balcony and ask for one of the quieter rooms that look out across a pretty garden to the rear of the building. But the highlight of a stay will be getting to grips with Casa García's traditional *onubense* cuisine. Many ingredients come fresh from the village *huertas*, the pork, ham and sausages are of the best and the decoration, bright and fresh, is conducive to a memorable and leisurely meal. There is a beautiful circular walk that leads straight out from the village: see my guide *Walking in Andalucía* for full route notes.

To see & do nearby: Visit to the old mezquita (mosque) in Almonaster, day trips to Portugal, walking in the Natural Park of Aracena.

MOLINO RÍO ALÁJAR

Finca Cabeza del Molino s/n, 21340 Alájar

Tel: 959 501 282

Email: molinorioalajar@telefonica.net

www.molinorioalajar.com

Management:	Monica de Vos & Peter Jan Mulder
Closed:	Never
Bedrooms:	6 Houses sleeping 2-6
Prices:	House for 2 €90-112 weekly, House for 4-6 €135-180 weekly + 7% VAT. Minimum stay of 2 nights
Meals:	No meals available but a hamper can be provided on arrival with all the basics for €25-35

Directions: From Aracena follow signs to Alájar. Pass above Alájar on road towards Santa Ana then turn left at signs for Ermita de San Bartolomé. Cross bridge then after 50 metres right then follow very narrow track to Molino Rio Alájar.

Huelva Province · Map 1 · HOTEL 004

Ancient cobbled footpaths and bridle ways wind through the hills west of Aracena, linking some of Andalucía's prettiest villages. My personal favourite is Alájar whose twisting, narrow alleyways are dominated by the lofty mountain chapel of Arias Montero. Just below the village is a converted mill which matches the village in its charm, as bucolic an idyll as you could hope to find. Monica and Peter, the Dutch owners, have built six cottages just up the hillside from the original mill house in a beautiful swathe of wooded hillside. The houses exude a warmth born of their dark chestnut beams, honey-coloured walls and handmade terracotta floor tiles. All of the cottages are large enough for you to be entirely independent but if you're feeling sociable there's a huge guest lounge in the mill house where there are masses of books, magazines and Peter's notes for several different walks leading straight out from the farm (or get hold of a copy of Santana's *Walking in Andalucía*). You can also cover the same footpaths by donkey with a local guide. Although this place is set up for self-catering a welcome hamper of goodies can be provided and you're welcome to pick veggies from the Molino's garden. Be prepared to negotiate a narrow, walled track if arriving by car.

To see & do nearby: Walking and riding, visits to villages of the Sierra, day trips to Portugal and Sevilla.

LA POSADA DE ALÁJAR

Calle Médico Emilio González 2, 21340 Alájar

Tel: 959 125 712 or 667 906 132

Email: info@laposadadealajar.com

www.laposadadealajar.com

Management:	Lucy Arkwright & Angel Millán Simó
Closed:	January
Bedrooms:	4 Twins, 4 Doubles and 1 Apartment
Prices:	Double/Twin €60, Apartment for 4 €120 including VAT
Meals:	Breakfast included, Picnic €10, Dinner €20 excluding wine, by prior arrangement

Directions: From Sevilla north on A66/E803 towards Mérida then N433 towards Portugal to Aracena. Continue towards Portugal then left for Fuenteheridos. At roundabout left following signs Alájar and La Peña. At the next junction turn right then after 1 km go left into village. The hotel is on left before you reach the square.

Alájar is the jewel in the crown of the Aracena park, a tiny village of cobbled streets dominated by the extraordinary Arias Montero peak. Just yards from the village's main square La Posada would be a good base for forays into the park if simple, unaffected comfort is enough for you. At the turn of the century it was known as the Bar de las Estacas, an allusion to the wooden pegs where muleteers would hang their blankets and saddle bags. Lucy and Angel have given La Posada a thorough refurbishment, bringing new life to this simple hostelry. Most of the bedrooms are quite small with carpetted floors and have shower rooms with cork floors of similarly reduced proportions. Bright colours and Angel's photos - on display throughout the house - add a dash of personality. The nicest part of La Posada is its beamed and slate-floored lounge, a lovely spot to unwind before dinner, in front of the fire in winter. Expect to eat well, most of what is on your plate will have been locally sourced, and a big breakfast is served. If you prefer to eat out there are a couple of good restaurants just along the road. My personal favourite is Bar La Parra where you can feast on wild mushrooms when in season. *The Posada doubles as an information point for the Sierra de Aracena Natural Park.*

To see & do nearby: The Rio Tinto Mines, walking and riding in the Aracena Natural Park, day trips to Portugal.

FINCA BUEN VINO

Los Marines, 21293 Aracena

Tel: 959 124 034 Fax: 959 501 029

Email: availability@fincabuenvino.com

www.fincabuenvino.com

Management:	Jeannie & Sam Chesterton
Closed:	Christmas & New Year
Bedrooms:	4 Doubles and 3 Cottages with their own pools
Prices:	Double €135-150 for shorter stays, €120-135 for longer stays, Cottages €1000 weekly high season or from €400 weekly low season + 7% VAT
Meals:	Breakfast included, Dinner €42.50 including wine

Directions: From Sevilla north on A66/E803 towards Mérida then branch onto N433 towards Portugal. Bypass Aracena and village of Los Marines and look for sign for Buen Vino approx. 1.5 kms after Los Marines at km 95 post turn right into the estate.

Huelva Province · Map 1 · HOTEL 006

Buen Vino – just writing those two words evokes the happiest memories of a number of stays at one of Andalucía's most seductive country retreats. This elegant country home - you'd never guess that it is only twenty years old – stands alone in a beautiful swathe of chestnut and oak forest. And home this is, rather than hotel. A stay with Sam and Jeannie is all about becoming a part of a ready-made, supremely convivial house party. There isn't the tiniest hint of chain hotel here: each bedroom is different to the next with stacks of paintings, magazines, books and individual decorative flourishes. Downstairs a cosy, panelled dining room provides a perfect setting for Jeannie's gourmet suppers. The food is fantastic, the wine superb and the Chestertons are relaxed, entertaining hosts. There's a beautiful pool tucked a discrete distance from the house with a stunning canopy view of the forest. Book a week's stay in one of the cottages if you're really keen to commune, in great comfort, with nature and be sure to fit in some walking: there are ancient footpaths all around and Sam knows the best of them. And call Jeannie for details of the cookery courses that she organises at Buen Vino. *Wireless internet access throughout the house and in cottages, too.*

To see & do nearby: Visits to the 'Gruta de las Maravillas' cave in Aracena and the villages of the Aracena Park, swimming and picnics at the reservoirs.

EL CORTIJO DE LOS MIMBRALES

Ctra del Rocío A-483 km 30,5, 21750 Almonte

Tel: 959 442 237 Fax: 959 442 443

Email: info@cortijomimbrales.com

www.cortijomimbrales.com

Management:	Andrés Abrines
Closed:	Never
Bedrooms:	12 Doubles, 14 Twins and 6 Cottages sleeping 2 or 4
Prices:	Standard Double/Twin €100, Superior Double/Twin €125, Cottage for 2 €195, Cottage for 4 €270 + 7% VAT
Meals:	Breakfast included, Lunch/Dinner €30-35 including wine.

Directions: From Sevilla west on the A49 motorway towards Portugal. Exit for Bolullos del Condado and follow A483 towards Almonte/Malalascañas. The hotel is on the right 5 kms past El Rocío.

Huelva Province · Map 1 · HOTEL 007

If you've journeyed to El Rocío you'll know that the Doñana National Park has a unique beauty which somehow makes it feel like a world apart from the rest of Andalucía. Just a five minute drive from the larger-than-life Rocío sanctuary and its languid lagoon is one of southern Spain's most striking small hotels. The outside of this low, hacienda-style building – it lies at the heart of a vast citrus plantation – is appealing enough but it is the striking use of colour within that is so attractive and original: ochre, sienna, cobalt blue and terracotta. Everywhere your eye comes to rest there's a visual feast – all that colour, exuberant roses, ferns and jasmine, a seductive commingling of antique furnishing and fabulous contemporary works of art. You choose between a room or a cottage: all are four-star comfortable and have been decorated with the same decorative flair. The night after staying here I made a long journey back to eat a second meal in Los Mimbrales' beautiful, high-ceilinged restaurant, La Cantina. The combination of great food and décor, good-natured, efficient service make a stay here an unforgettable experience. The extraordinary Rocío sanctuary is just along the road, there are great beaches nearby and the birdlife here is unforgettable. So don't forget your field guide and binoculars!

To see & do nearby: Visits to the Doñana National Park, the sanctuary of the El Rocío Virgin, watersports and beaches.

HOTEL TORUÑO

Plaza Acebuchal 22, 21750 El Rocío

Tel: 959 442 626 or 959 442 323 Fax: 959 442 338

Email: hoteltoruno@eresmas.com

www.toruno.es

Management:	Andés Pérez
Closed:	Never
Bedrooms:	7 Doubles and 23 Twins.
Prices:	Double/Twin €79-125 + 7% VAT. Prices increase enormously during any of the Rocío festivities: check!
Meals:	Breakfast included, Picnic €12, Lunch/Dinner at adjacent sister restaurant €15 including wine

Directions: From Sevilla west on A49 towards Portugal then exit for Bollullos del Condado. Then follow A483 towards Almonte/Malalascañas to El Rocío. The hotel is 200 yards behind the Rocío Sanctuary.

All estate agents and hoteliers tell you it's all about one thing: location. And the 'l' factor comes no higher than at El Toruño. It is just a hundred yards from the shrine of the Rocío Virgin, plumb in the centre of the vast Doñana reserve and just yards from the lagoon which brings ornithologists flocking from all over the world. I'll never forget awaking to a blushing dawn and seeing the outline of several dozen flamingos gradually sharpen as a languid February sun burned off the early morning mist. Be sure to get a room with a view. The best, number 225, has windows on two sides and all odd-numbered rooms between 207 and 217 catch a part of that incredible vista. Each bedroom is dedicated to a different species of bird and even in the bathrooms there are hand-painted pictures of things feathered. All of them are as clean as clean can be. You eat in a sister restaurant just across the way, perhaps in the shade of the huge, wild olive trees which grow outside. Specialities include fish and organic beef raised in the Doñana reserve. A unique village which out of season feels like a deserted Wild West town. And a unique hotel.

To see & do nearby: Visits to the Doñana National Park, the Sanctuary of the El Rocío Virgin, beaches.

HOTELS 009 – 020

SEVILLA

CASA Nº 7

Calle Virgenes 7, 41004 Sevilla

Tel: 954 221 581 Fax: 954 214 527

Email: info@casanumero7.com

www.casanumero7.com

Management:	Gonzalo del Río y González-Gordon
Closed:	Never
Bedrooms:	4 Doubles and 2 Twins
Prices:	Double/Twin €177-275 + 7% VAT
Meals:	Breakfast included, no other meals. Huge choice of bars and restaurants close to hotel.

Directions: Park in any city centre car park. The nearest is 'Cano y Cueto' at the junction of Calle Cano y Cueto and Menéndez Pelayo. Then take a taxi to the hotel.

Recently selected by the British magazine Tatler as its 'Small Hotel of the Year' there's nowhere to stay in Sevilla quite like Casa No.7. A host of details give away a certain nostalgia for the Noel Coward era: scrambled eggs (in olive oil) at breakfast, a white-jacketed butler to whisk your suitcase up to your room and an elegant drawing room where you are served a glass of chilled *fino* before you head out for dinner. And it will be the best of *fino*: Gonzalo's family are the owners of González-Byass and he knows a thing or two about good sherry. Comfort and elegance are the keynotes of the bedrooms he created at Casa No 7. Liberty-esque fabrics, rugs, antique dressers, framed prints and oil paintings, family photographs and books give them a feel that is both homely and elegant. Marble floors, airconditioning and high ceilings provide an effective foil to Seville's long hot summer and much of the appeal of staying here is that Casa No. 7 feels like a privileged inner sanctum, hidden away from the heat and rumble of the Andalusian capital. With luck you may meet Gonzalo and share conversation about changing times in the sherry trade. Like a certain Jeeves, both he and his hotel are inimitable.

To see & do nearby: The Cathedral and the Giralda, the Jewish Quarter, the Plaza de España, the María Luisa Park.

HOTEL ALMINAR

Calle Alvárez Quintero 52, 41004 Sevilla

Tel: 954 293 913 Fax: 954 212 197
Email: reservas@hotelalminar.com
www.hotelalminar.com

Management:	Francisco Naranjo Peral
Closed:	Never
Bedrooms:	2 Singles, 6 Twins, 2 Doubles and 2 Suites
Prices:	Single €60-95, Twin Double €90-125, Suite €110-155 + 7% VAT
Meals:	Breakfast €6

Directions: Calle Alvárez Quintero is just to the east of the cathedral. Best to leave car in either Plaza Nueva car park or Puerta de Jerez car park then take taxi to hotel.

Alminar's position could hardly be better: plumb in the centre of Seville, just 50 metres from its elephantine gothic cathedral and a short stroll from the Plaza Nueva and Calle Sierpes. The hotel has earned a good reputation for being a comfortable, reliable place to overnight and, above all, a friendly one. All that remains of the original edifice is its elegant sandy-coloured facade, the rest having been completely renovated in order to create the 12 bedrooms and small inner patio-cum-reception. Space is at a premium at breakfast but luckily you can have it delivered to your room which is especially tempting if you have one of those on the top floor which look across the rooftops to the Giralda. I'd be tempted forego the hotel's breakfast and head out to a lively bar for coffee and *tostadas*. All bedrooms are double-glazed and have a vaguely Zen/Eighties feel: dark wood, subtle lighting and hi-tech shower rooms which make the most of limited space. Best of all is the easy, good nature of Francisco ('Paco') and his staff. Heed their restaurant and bar recommendations if you're keen to discover some great, non-touristy spots. It was thanks to Paco that I got to know La Estrella which has since become one of my favourite Andalusian *tapas* bars.

To see & do nearby: The Cathedral and Giralda, the Santa Cruz district, flamenco bars and peñas in Triana.

LAS CASAS DEL REY DE BAEZA

Calle Santiago, Plaza Jesús de la Redención, 41003 Sevilla

Tel: 954 561 496 or 902 254 255 Fax: 954 561 441

Email: lascasasdelreydebaeza@hospes.es

www.fuenso.es

Management:	Cristina Álvarez
Closed:	Never
Bedrooms:	30 Doubles, 6 Twins and 5 Suites
Prices:	Double/Twin €165-210, Suite €300-400 + 7% VAT. At Feria and Easter prices approx. double those of low season.
Meals:	Breakfast €17, Lunch/Dinner from €40

Directions: The hotel is close to both the Iglesia de Santa Catalina and the Casa de Pilatos. Nearest car park is Escuelas Pias. If lost just ask any taxi driver to guide you to Escuelas Pias.

Sevilla Province · Map 2 · HOTEL 011

Sevilla's many *patios de vecinos* could be likened to early tenement blocks: those who worked for its more illustrious families were lodged in these purpose-built edifices so that they'd be close to the grand homes that they served. This particular one was given as a present by King Fernando II to one of his faithful knights. What were once small family homes have now become elegant bedrooms thanks to an inspired restoration which, like so many others in Sevilla, took place just before the '92 Expo. The mood of Las Casas is subdued and refined, a cool mix of contemporary colours, fittings and design with the traditional backdrop of a cobbled, columned and galleried patio. There's a wonderful drawing room with masses of leather sofas and armchairs, interesting lamps, contemporary art and all of it is given an extra lift thanks to the light which filters in from it's high French windows. Elegant black slate and subtle pastel shades set the mood in bedrooms. These have a host of extras like CD, DVD and wifi as well as goodies galore in the bathrooms. Have a sandwich up by the rooftop pool, indulge in a massage in the *Bodyna* spa, dine on *cocina andaluza creativa* in the excellent restaurant and find time to visit the nearby Casa de Pilatos and its exquisite gardens.

To see & do nearby: La Casa de Pilatos, the María Luisa Park, the Bellas Artes museum, the Santa Cruz area.

CORRAL DEL REY

Corral del Rey 12, 41004 Sevilla

Tel: 954 227 116 Fax: 954 226 389
Email: info@corraldelrey.com
www.corraldelrey.com

Management:	Anthony & Patrick Reed Moro-Figueroa
Closed:	Never
Bedrooms:	2 Superior Double, 2 Deluxe Double and 2 Junior Suites
Prices:	Superior Double €280, Deluxe Double €320, Junior Suite €350 + 7% VAT
Meals:	Dinner approx. €35-40 à la carte. Restaurant closed on Monday nights.

Directions: Corral del Rey is in the Alfalfa district, close to the Plaza de la Alfalfa. The nearest car parks are Cano y Cueto in Menéndez-Pelayo or Plaza Real. From both car parks it is just a short taxi ride to the hotel or a five minute walk.

Anthony and Patrick Reed have already made big waves at the Hacienda de San Rafael, a chic rural retreat just south of Sevilla. Corral del Rey, their latest venture, is the country hotel's *media naranja*, it's perfect partner. The hotel was born out of the meticulous restoration of a 17th century mansion house which stands at the heart of Seville's narcotic old town, just out of the tourist shadow yet less than a five minute stroll from the Cathedral. This is 'boutique' hotel at its boutiquey best: just six guest rooms, great food and service that turns caring into an art form. It begins at the door when your bag is whisked across the atrium-topped patio and up to your room where a bottle of *fino* and a handwritten note of welcome await you. Kuky Reed has waved her unique decorative wand to create a mood of cool, cossetted comfort. Fabrics are by Nicole Fabré, lighting by Lutron, there are bespoke cabinets for the sound and TV system, queen size beds and bathrooms fit for a king decked out in limestone and marble. And the Corral's restaurant, which doubles as an art gallery, is fabulous: glass-topped tables lined up diner-style in front of a long, striped bench seat and a 'less is more' menu offering four starters, mains and deserts: my dinner was superb. On the roof terrace there's a small plunge pool with a view of the Giralda: I'd breakfast here and drink in those cityscape views in the morning sunlight.

To see & do nearby: The Santa Cruz and Triana areas, music at La Carbonería, the Casa de Pilatos and the Cathedral, gardens and river trips.

ALCOBA DEL REY DE SEVILLA

Bécquer 9, 41002 Sevilla

Tel: 954 915 800 Fax: 954 915 675
Email: info@alcobadelrey.com
www.alcobadelrey.com

Management:	Rafael Carrión Amate
Closed:	Never
Bedrooms:	4 Standard Twin/Doubles, 3 Superior Twin/Doubles and 8 Junior Suites
Prices:	Standard Double/Twin €125-150, Superior Double/Twin €146-180, Junior Suite €167-200 + 7% VAT
Meals:	Breakfast included

Directions: The hotel is just to the east of the Macarena church. Best to stop a taxi and let it guide you to the hotel. The hotel has a (paying) car park in Calle Bécquer shortly before you reach the hotel: ring reception for details. Or park in any city centre car park and taxi to hotel.

In the shadow of the basilica of Santa María de la Esperanza Macarena, home to Seville's most venerated Virgin, La Alcoba is one of a growing number of small Andalusian hotels that look to North Africa for decorative inspiration. From the outside the hotel looks much like any other 19th century *sevillano* town house but once you're inside you feel as if you've been magicked away to the souk in Tangier. Mirrors, lamps, crockery, low tables, silk cushions (all for sale!) were shipped back across the Strait to create a corner of Morocco in Spain. A trickling fountain, keyhole arches, ornate stucco moldings and a *haima* (wedding tent) on the roof terrace further enhance the atmosphere, at times a wee bit kitschy, of The 1001 Nights. Each of Alcoba's bedrooms is named after a figure of the Moorish period. They vary greatly in size but all have big beds draped in bright *sabra* silks with intricately carved cedar headboards, tables, desks and chairs. Bathrooms are just as festive with shining polished stucco, beaten copper basins and handsome repro taps from India: yes, even these are up for the grabs! Breakfast is served around low tables leading off from the patio whilst at other times of day a selection of drinks and *tapas*, inspired by the flavours of the Maghreb, are on offer in the hotel's colourful bar.

To see & do nearby: The Macarena church, the Isla Mágica, boat trips on the Guadalquivir, flamenco in Triana, wandering Sevilla's historic centre.

LA CARTUJA DE CAZALLA

Ctra Cazalla - Constantina A-455 km 2,5, 41370 Cazalla de la Sierra

Tel: 954 884 516 Fax: 954 884 707

Email: info@cartujadecazalla.com

www.cartujadecazalla.com

. . . .

Management:	Carmen Ladrón de Guevara
Closed:	December 24 & 25
Bedrooms:	2 Singles, 2 Doubles, 4 Twins, 4 Suites and 2 Cottages
Prices:	Single €62, Double/Twin €100, Suite €135, Cottage €160 + 7% VAT. Minimum stay of 2 nights in cottages.
Meals:	Breakfast included, Lunch/Dinner €28 including wine

. . . .

Directions: From Sevilla A431 to Cantillana. Here take the A432 via El Pedroso to Cazalla. Follow signs through town for Constantina. After leaving the town on A455 continue 2.5 kms then turn left at sign for La Cartuja.

It is impossible to imagine what confronted Carmen de Ladrón de Guevara when some three decades back she happened upon this crumbling Carthusian monastery. She didn't simply hope to rescue these ancient stones but also breathe new artistic and spiritual life into a building whose physical setting seems to lift you above the mundane and inspire you to greater things. Hundreds of lorry-loads of rubble were cleared away and the shape and structure of the original buildings gradually reemerged from the dense foliage that had engulfed the building. You stay in what were the monk's cells, in the annex that Carmen hailed as 'a building for the New Millennium' almost a decade back, or in one of the newly built cottages. The silence at night, the extraordinary chapel, and dinner with Carmen make for a totally unique experience. Thanks to her single-mindedness La Cartuja has become a forum for artistic debate and a scenario for the creative impulse: you may well coincide with a concert, an exhibition of painting or some theatrical event. There are fabulous walks straight out from La Cartuja, including a marked walk around the estate and the nearby village of Cazalla has a charm all of its own. Carmen has recently written the story of her love affair with La Cartuja: copies of the book are on sale in reception.

To see & do nearby: Visits to the Huesnar river valley, day trips to Sevilla and Écija, exploring the Cartuja's estate, reading and painting.

LAS NAVEZUELAS

A-432 km 43,5, Apartado de Correos 14 , 41370 Cazalla de la Sierra

Tel: 954 884 764 Fax: 954 884 594

Email: navezuela@arrakis.es

www.lasnavezuelas.com

Management:	Luca Cicorella
Closed:	January 3 – February 27
Bedrooms:	1 Double, 3 Twins, 2 Suites, 3 Apartments for 2, 2 Apartments for 4 and 1 Apartment for 6
Prices:	Double/Twin €60-65, Suite €75-80, Apartment for 2 €87-95, Apartment for 4 €120-130, Apartment for 6 €150 + 7% VAT
Meals:	Breakfast included (not for apartment), Lunch/Dinner €20 (ex.wine). Summer: lunches only, Winter: dinners only.

Directions: From Sevilla A8006 to Cantillana. Here take the A432 via El Pedroso towards Cazalla. Pass km 43 marker post, continue for 500 metres then turn right and follow track to Las Navezuelas.

Luca and his wife Mariló were making waves at Las Navezuelas long before the phrase *turismo rural* had entered the vernacular. Thanks to their vision this small country hotel is now considered a benchmark for young folk with similar aspirations and has won a number of awards. The setting is deeply bucolic, a low whitewashed *lagar* with nothing to interrupt a sweeping panorama of farmland which stretches away for miles and miles - apart from the occasional flock of sheep or goats. The decoration of bedrooms and communal space is fresh, simple and rustic and the overall feel of Las Navezuelas is uncluttered and soothing, the sort of place that would inspire you to put a pen to paper or to reach for the sketch pad. And the food philosophy is similar to the decorative one: traditional and wholesome with no airs of grandeur. Guests return here year after year as does the stork that nests on a rooftop turret. Wake to birdsong, breakfast to Bach, dine to good flamenco music: an aural as well as a visual feast awaits you. So be sure to book at least two nights at this delectable address and find time to visit Cazalla and to hike in the Sierra del Norte Park: the Huesnar river valley walk is particularly memorable.

To see & do nearby: Visits to the Huesnar river valley, the Sierra del Viento for panoramic views of the Sierra, the villages of Cazalla and El Pedroso.

EL TRIGUERO

Ctra Carmona - El Viso del Alcor N-398 km 18, 41410 Carmona

Tel: 955 953 626 or 626 056 323 Fax: 955 953 626

Email: reservaseltriguero@valmenta.com

www.eltriguero.com

Management:	Carmen Vega Salguero
Closed:	Never
Bedrooms:	3 Doubles and 7 Twins
Prices:	Double/Twin €55-60 + 7% VAT
Meals:	Breakfast included, Dinner €18 including wine, by prior arrangement.

Directions: From Carmona N392 towards El Viso del Alcor (also signposted for 'Lidl' supermarket)). At km 29 marker post turn left and follow track to El Triguero.

There are still places to stay in Andalucía where simple comfort takes precedence over satellite TV and jacuzzi bath tubs. If you're happy to sleep far from shops, bars and the rumble of traffic, if you don't mind swapping a gleaming hotel reception for a kindly housekeeper called Carmen whose English is of the "good...please?" variety, if you're happy with simple country cooking rather than burgers and pizza, this should be your type of place. This alluring *cortijo* stands alone on a low ridge looking out across mile after mile of farmland, the breadbasket of Sevilla. Seeing the sunset here and feeling the silence of the night wrap around the house is an experience never to be forgotten: be sure to find time for a walk through the estate by way of the sandy citrus grove that laps up to the main house. And the overall atmosphere at El Triguero is far more that of a home than a hotel. There are cut flowers, family portraits and photographs, etchings and oil paintings and simple yet elegant bedrooms with fans to keep the heat at bay. I'd try to book the tower room and combine a stay here with a few leisurely evening outings to Carmona which remains unsullied by tourism yet has an enchanting town centre and some great restaurants, too.

To see & do nearby: Visits to Carmona, Sevilla and Osuna, great local bars and restaurants, walking in the Sierra del Norte.

HOTEL PALACIO DE LOS GRANADOS

Calle Emilio Castelar 42, 41400 Écija

Tel: 955 901 050 Fax: 955 905 344

Email: info@palaciogranados.com

www.palaciogranados.com

Management:	Francisco Ortíz de la Renta & Pablo Ojeda O'Neill
Closed:	Never
Bedrooms:	4 Twins, 6 Doubles and 4 Suites
Prices:	Double/Twin €154-187, Suite €187-232 including VAT
Meals:	Breakfast included, gourmet Dinner €55-60, by prior arrangement.

Directions: From Sevilla toward Madrid on A4/E5. Exit at km 455 for Écija/Osuna then follow signs for 'centro urbano'. You will soon pick up signs for 'Palacio de los Granados' which is at the far end of Calle Emilio Castelar on the right. Hotel has own parking next door.

Never part of the Andalusian 'Grand Tour' Écija has rarely attracted travellers in great numbers: perhaps its reputation as being the *sartén de Andalucía* (the frying pan of the South!) deterred would-be visitors . Yet this is one of the most ancient towns in Andalucía, surrounded by fertile farmlands and christened by the Moors *Ishtiya* or 'rich town'. After suffering extensive damage in the 1755 earthquake the town was rebuilt in grandiose Baroque style. El Palacio de los Granados is one of several mansions that date back to that period and was nursed back to life by Francisco and Pablo, two multi-talented architect/interior decorators from Puerto Rico. The palace embraces a central courtyard with a double tier of arches and columns, murmuring fountain and ancient flags whilst in a second courtyard pomegranates and citrus trees overhang a fountain-fed pool. The suites and bedrooms lead off from the patios on two floors and have been decorated in a sumptuous style that mirrors that of the building's antique-packed public spaces, marrying *mudéjar* and classical elements: they are narcotic, Andalusian and a wee bit theatrical, too. Treat yourself to a splendid dinner, abandon yourself to the Andalusian night and be thankful that Los Granados, Écija and its fascinating historical centre are yet to be discovered by the lumpen.

To see & do nearby: Day trips to Sevilla and Córdoba, the old centre of Écija, walking and riding in the Sierra del Norte.

HOTEL PALACIO MARQUÉS DE LA GOMERA

Calle San Pedro 20, 41640 Osuna

Tel: 954 812 223 Fax: 954 810 200

Email: info@hotelpalaciodelmarques.com

www.hotelpalaciodelmarques.com

Management:	Francisco Álvarez
Closed:	Never
Bedrooms:	17 Twin/Doubles, 1 Superior Double and 2 Suites
Prices:	Standard Double/Twin €99-110, Superior Double €116-130, Suite €161-185 + 7% VAT. Prices slightly higher Easter/Feria.
Meals:	Breakfast €10, Lunch/Dinner €30-35 inc. wine. Patio restaurant (summer) approx. €20. Restaurants shut Tuesdays.

Directions: From Sevilla take A92 towards Granada then first exit for Osuna. At roundabout straight ahead, up Calle Sevilla to Plaza Mayor. Exit at top left of square into Calle Carrera. First left after Calle San Pedro, then second left and left again to hotel.

One of the best things about exploring inland Andalucía is happening upon exquisite towns and villages that get virtually no press yet whose beauty can take your breath away. Osuna had this effect on me when I first visited and was simply bowled over by its Calle San Pedro and its remarkable hotel, El Marqués de la Gomera. After a dusty drive across the wheatlands east of Sevilla the opulence of its flamboyant portal, its marbled patio and imposing sweep of baroque staircase leaves you wondering: why Osuna? The building's base element is the warm, golden sandstone that is so characteristic of the town's architecture. The most remarkable of Gomera's bedrooms is the Torreón suite: from its lofty perch you have a panoramic roofscape view of the whole of the old centre of Osuna. But all rooms are special, most of them cavernous, and are decorated with a successful commingling of antiques and contemporary furnishings. Bed linen, mattresses and fabrics are top-of-the-range and bathrooms big, with piles of monogrammed towels and flannels. At lunch or dinner you choose between two restaurants: the one in the garden has a more informal feel, offering just *tapas* and *raciones* whilst the Casa del Marqués has grander airs and is more focused on gourmet cuisine. So why Osuna? In the 17th century it became the pivotal point of trade in the area and home to the most entrepreneurial of the western Andalusian nobility.

To see & do nearby: Visits to Sevilla, Écija and Córdoba, exploring the old centre of Osuna, lively tapas bars and restaurants.

HACIENDA DE SAN RAFAEL

Apartado de Correos 28, Ctra Nacional IV km 594,
41730 Las Cabezas de San Juan

Tel: 955 872 193 Fax: 955 872 201
Email: info@haciendadesanrafael.com
www.haciendadesanrafael.com

Management:	Patrick & Anthony Reed
Closed:	November 15 – March 15
Bedrooms:	7 Doubles, 4 Twins and 3 Cottages
Prices:	Double/Twin €225, Casita €480 + 7% VAT. Whole property can be hired for celebrations: details on request.
Meals:	Breakfast included, Lunch approx. €30, Dinner €55 ex. wine.

Directions: Leave Sevilla following signs for Cádiz and just before you reach the motorway branch onto the NIV. Shortly before Las Cabezas de San Juan, just past km 594 marker post (be sure to keep well to right and indicate!), turn right and follow long drive to San Rafael.

The rolling farmlands stretching south from Sevilla have a unique beauty, a vast, open landscape peppered with whitewashed farmsteads over which high, swaying palms stand sentinel. San Rafael is every inch the classic Andalusian *cortijo*, surrounded by olive groves and with an ochre and white facade giving onto to an inner courtyard awash with brilliant damask bougainvillaea. Thanks to the decorative nous and *savoir faire* of the Reed family it is has been transformed into one of Andalucía's most exceptional small hotels, successfully fusing things Spanish with more exotic, eastern notes. Choose between a *casita* (three share their own pool) or one of the mezzanine rooms. They have masses of space, walk-in bathrooms and their own verandahs. There are masses of hidden corners for chilling out at San Rafael and this is very much a place for the Big (and pampered) Relax. Start the evening with an *aperitivo* in the sunset bar, have a fabulous candle-lit dinner in the courtyard or the east garden, then while away a few hours star-gazing in the lunar bar. The Reed brothers are keen to take San Rafael to new places and there's a definite debt in mood and decor to the exclusive hotel hideaways that their father manages in the Far East.

To see & do nearby: Visits to the Sherry bodegas in Jerez, the city of Sevilla, and the Doñana Park.

ALGUACILES BAJOS

Ctra Las Cabezas de San Juan - Montellano A-8128 km 3,3
41710 Las Cabezas de San Juan

Tel: 630 561 529 Fax: 915 641 071

Email: alguaciles@alguaciles.com
www.alguaciles.com

Management:	Simón Carrero
Closed:	August 1-15, September 1-15
Bedrooms:	1 Single, 1 Double and 6 Twins
Prices:	Single €48, Double/Twin €60 including VAT and contents of your mini-bar.
Meals:	Breakfast included. 2 simple *ventas* close by.

Directions: From Sevilla NIV to Cabezas de San Juan. Exit to right at km 594 for Villamartín and follow the A371 towards Villamartín. After approx. 6.5 kms turn left again on A8128 towards Montellano. A. Bajos is on the left after 3.3 kms.

Sevilla Province · Map 2 · HOTEL 020

If you're tiring of the tourist-beaten track and are keen to get a real feel for life on an Andalusian *cortijo* book a couple of nights at Alguaciles Bajos. The farm is lost in the gently rolling hills of the Sevilla *campiña*, girdled by a belt of tall palm trees, miles from the nearest village. Entering the farm's 400 year-old cobbled courtyard is like stepping back into another age. Expect no uniformed receptionist to greet you here. Instead, the ever-smiling farm manager Simon emerges to show you to your room. It will be vast, with old and modern paintings, sofa, easy chairs, a comfortable bed, sparkling bathroom and even air-conditioning and a fridge. Once you've unpacked and marveled at your room (what incredible value!) be sure to follow a way-marked path out across the estate, through fields of wheat and sunflowers. At sunset this is an exquisite experience. Then drive just a mile or two along the narrowest of country lanes to a simple little *venta* where you won't hear anything apart from Spanish being spoken, and very loudly of course. You'll feel a million miles away from Marbella and, if you're like me, be thankful that there are still places in Spain which are truly different.

To see & do nearby: Sevilla, Jerez and the white villages of the Grazalema Natural Park, painting and reading at the farm.

HOTELS 021 – 047

CÁDIZ

POSADA DE PALACIO

Calle Caballeros 11, 11540 Sanlúcar de Barrameda

Tel: 956 364 840 Fax: 956 365 060

Email: posadadepalacio@terra.es

www.posadadepalacio.com

Management:	Ester & Federico Galera
Closed:	Mid January – mid February
Bedrooms:	10 Doubles, 11 Twins, 9 Suites and 2 Quadruples
Prices:	Double/Twin €75-90, Superior Double/Twin €95-120, Suite €120-150 + 7% VAT
Meals:	Breakfast €6

Directions: Arriving in Sanlúcar on A480 bear right at petrol station. At roundabout continue straight on and at next fork go left into Avenida Doctor Fleming. Pass Barbadillo bodega and Paroquía de la O. Posada is on the left.

Most visitors to Sanlúcar de Barrameda come to see the enormous bodegas where its dry *manzanilla* wine is produced. There are a host of other reasons for coming: to make a boat trip up the Guadalquivir, to visit Doñana National Park, to wander its lively covered markets, to eat fish and seafood fresh from the ocean and to visit a place which remains unscathed by mass tourism. And to stay at the delightful Posada de Palacio. This rambling mansion seems to encapsulate the mood of the town: sleepy, beguiling and with an air of former glories. An inner patio sets the mood: ferns, a well, old flagstones and classical *albero* ochre picking out detail on the elegant moldings. Each bedroom is different to the next, following the twists and turns of the building, some are vast, others smaller, a number have sitting rooms and balconies, but all are really nice. I always look forward to breakfast at La Posada: great coffee, freshly squeezed orange juice and the thought of a day in this wonderful town. The hotel has recently been revamped and redecorated from top to bottom and new bedrooms have been added in second house which has been linked in with the original posada. Be sure to stroll down the hill past the Cathedral, have a *manzanilla* in the charming Plaza del Cabildo, and relax into the mood of this beguiling town.

To see & do nearby: Visits to the Doñana Park, the Salinas (salt beds) & pine forests of Monte Algaida, *manzanilla* bodegas and the old town of Sanlúcar.

LOS HELECHOS

Plaza de Madre de Dios 9, 11540 Sanlúcar de Barrameda

Tel: 956 361 349 or 956 367 655 Fax: 956 369 650

Email: info@hotelloshelechos.com

www.hotelloshelechos.com

Management:	Manuel Reina de los Reyes
Closed:	Never
Bedrooms:	8 Doubles and 46 Twins
Prices:	Double/Twin €54-71 + 7% VAT
Meals:	Breakfast €5, no Lunch/Dinner available apart from snacks in the cafeteria. Several good fish bars and restaurants within walking distance.

Directions: From Jerez A480 to Sanlúcar. Here take Avenida del Vº Centenario following signs 'Centro Ciudad'. Los Helechos is in the lower part of old town in Calle Baños. If lost ask for Plazaleta de La Salle.

Another Sanlúcar hotel which oozes Andalucía from its every corner, Los Helechos is the fruit of the complete renovation of a turn-of-the century mansion. You enter via a massive oak door which leads through to a marble-flagged patio with geometric tiles, wrought-iron grilles, whitewashed walls and masses of potted ferns, from which the hotel takes its name. In the hotel's reception you're greeted by a statue of the Rocío Virgin and a friendly receptionist. The bedrooms, which are nothing grand but perfectly comfortable, are reached via a series of patios where lemon trees, potted aspidistra and murmuring fountains strike the same southern note. Most look in towards the patios and those giving on to the street are double-glazed to reduce the noise of passing traffic. The rooms are medium-sized, simply furnished, sparkling clean and the best retain their original floor tiles. From Los Helechos you have just a short stroll to the town's delightful palm-fringed square, the Plaza del Cabildo. No visit to the town is complete without a *tapa de tortilla de camarones* (shrimps deep-fried in batter) at Casa Balbino which is much more appealing than the hotel's rather garish caféteria. And if you're feeling like a really great dinner head on to Bigotes or Paco Segundino in Bajo de Guía.

To see & do nearby: Visits to The Doñana Park, the Salinas salt beds, the pine forest of Monte Algaida, the old town of Sanlúcar and the *manzanilla* bodegas.

HOSPEDERÍA DUQUES DE MEDINA SIDONIA

Plaza Condes de Niebla 1, 11540 Sanlúcar de Barrameda

Tel: 956 360 161 Fax: 956 369 608

Email: archivo@fcmedinasidonia.com

www.ruralduquesmedinasidonia.com

Management:	Caridad López
Closed:	Never
Bedrooms:	2 Doubles, 7 Twins and 1 Suite
Prices:	Double €70-85, El Partido Suite €105-110 + 7% VAT
Meals:	Breakfast included, tapas & light lunches/dinners in cafetería approx. €20-25

Directions: Arriving in Sanlúcar on A480 bear right at petrol station. At roundabout continue straight on and at next fork go left into Avenida Doctor Fleming. Pass Barbadillo bodega and Paroquía de la O turn left at sign for Hopsedería. Drop bags then look for parking.

The Hospedería de Medina Sidonia breaks radically from the standard hotel mold. It was opened by the Duchess of Medina Sidonia whose family have owned this building for no less than 700 years. She did so as a means of preserving her family archives: profits from rooms and food fund the conservation of this unique historical treasure. Her ten guest bedrooms are secreted away in a far wing of the palace. Decorated with floral fabrics, old prints and numerous heirlooms they feel deliciously out-of-time: elegant yet homely they are the antithesis of chain hotel identi-rooms. All have big bathrooms, crisp linen, piles of snowy-white towels and are really quiet considering you're at the heart of the old town. The dining area and drawing room of the main house are just as refined: there's an amazing collection of tapestries and oil paintings as well as elegant wing-backed chairs and sofas. And leading off from the interconnected salons is a lively cafeteria, popular with the Sanlúcar intelligentsia, which serves *tapas* throughout the day. The patio garden, though, is what I most remember, a botanical feast of palm, plumbago, citrus, pomegranate and bougainvillaea. If you breakfast here on a sunny morning or end the day with a chilled *manzanilla* and a plate of olives you won't want to be anywhere else.

To see & do nearby: Trips up the Guadalquivir to see the Doñana Park and the Salinas salt beds, the pine forest of Monte Algaida, the old town of Sanlúcar, visits to the *manzanilla bodegas*.

HOTEL CASA GRANDE

Plaza de las Angustias 3, 11402 Jerez de la Frontera

Tel: 956 345 070 Fax: 956 336 148

Email: hotel@casagrande.com.es

www.casagrande.com.es

Management:	Monika Schröder
Closed:	Never
Bedrooms:	4 Singles, 9 Twins/Doubles and 2 Junior Suites
Prices:	Single €57-67, Double/Twin €77-93, Suite €98-108 + 7% VAT. During Holy Week and Feria prices approximately double
Meals:	Breakfast €8, no other meals but masses of choice for eating in Jerez.

Directions: Arriving in Jerez head for 'Centro Ciudad'. The hotel is to the northern side of La Plaza de las Angustias and is well signposted. Hotel will email more detailed instructions. Or simply park at any city centre car park and take a taxi to Casa Grande.

The Plaza de las Angustias is at the heart of the old centre of Jerez, within easy walking distance of its fabulous Alcázar, several sherry bodegas and a number of excellent bars and restaurants. The square reminded me of the French Riviera with its high palm trees, elegant street lamps and swooping pigeons. And so too the elegant façade of Casa Grande, designed by the same architect who built the town's Villa Marta theatre. You enter the hotel by way of a cool patio and reception area where a sweep of marble floor, fountain and masses of potted plants are a perfect foil to the summer heat. The bedrooms, decorated with an appealing mix of antique and repro furniture, lead off from an unusual pentagonal inner patio. This is where breakfast – a generous, buffet event – is served in the warmer months. Your room at Casa Grande comes with a full quota of creature comforts: large bed, airconditioning, TV, wifi, handsome fabrics and a decent sized bathroom. Downstairs is a small guest lounge, bar and library and there's a large roof terrace with loungers and wide views out across the city. Given the degree of comfort at Casa Grande prices are more than reasonable and Monika and her staff are on hand to help in every possible way.

To see & do nearby: The sherry bodegas, the Real Escuela de Arte Equestre and visits to Doñana from Sanlúcar de Barrameda.

HOTEL LA CHANCILLERÍA

Calle Chancillería 21, 11403 Jerez de la Frontera

Tel: 956 301 038 or 661 119 119 Fax: 956 301 038

Email: info@hotelchancilleria.com

www.hotelchancilleria.com

Management:	Joana Francis & Antonio Díaz
Closed:	Never
Bedrooms:	2 Singles, 4 Twins and 8 Doubles
Prices:	Single €67-70, Standard Double/Twin €90-95, Superior Double/Twin €95-100 including VAT. Rates higher in Feria and during Grand Prix Racing. Check www for details.
Meals:	Breakfast included, Lunch/Dinner Restaurant closed

Directions: Exit from A4 for Jerez Parque Empresarial then follow signs for 'Centro Ciudad'. At 8th set of lights by church go left into Calle Porvera then first right into Calle Chancilleria. Hotel is on left after approx. 200m.

Joana and Antonio left England for the deep South after falling in love with the labyrinthine old centre of Jerez. They staked their claim by converting two 19th century houses, close to the old city wall, into a supremely comfortable small hotel and restaurant. What sold them on the property was its walled garden: eating meals *al fresco* in a city centre hotel is a real treat. The renovation project followed a strict eco brief: a state-of-the-art solar installation, top spec insulation and a design that took account of orientation and air flow. Most of the fourteen bedrooms face the garden and, beyond the house's ancient back wall, the dome of the adjacent church. They are light and airy, furnished with angular contemporary furniture (a lot of it from that big Swedish shop), bright cushions and bedspreads and have swish tiled and stuccoed bathrooms. All have individually controlled heating systems, minibars and wifi. And further treats await in Chancillería's *Sabores* restaurant (open to non-residents) where Juande is at the helm. He adds a creative twist to the time-tried recipes of inland and coastal Cádiz and his wine menu also looks to the best of what is local including, *claro*, those of Jerez. Your breakfast is a moveable feast, served in the restaurant, your room, the garden or up on the roof terrace looking out across the old town's rooftops.

To see & do nearby: The sherry bodegas and Escuela de Arte Equestre, day trips to Doñana from Sanlúcar de Barrameda, Atlantic Coast beaches less than an hour away.

HOTEL BELLAS ARTES

Plaza del Arroyo 49, 11402 Jerez de la Frontera

Tel: 956 348 430 Fax: 956 169 633

Email: reservas@hotelbellasartes.e.telefonica.net

www.hotelbellasartes.com

Management:	María José García
Closed:	Never
Bedrooms:	18 Twin/Doubles and 1 Suite
Prices:	Double/Twin €90-120, 'Honeymoon' Suite €120-150 + 7% VAT
Meals:	Breakfast included.

Directions: Hotel on north side of the Plaza del Arroyo, immediately opposite the Cathedral. Navigating through the centre of Jerez can be difficult: let a taxi guide you to Bellas Artes where there is space to offload luggage. The hotel has its own car park (additional charge).

If you're looking to sleep in style at the centre of the old Jerez then look no further. This small boutique hotel, born out of an award-winning restoration of an 18th century mansion house, looks out across the leafy Plaza del Arroyo to the city's magnificent gothic cathedral: the hotel's façade, with its exquisitely carved cornicing and entrance portal, seems to vie with the decoration of the religious edifice. The same self-conscious elegance is reflected in the hotel's inner patio where a broad sweep of marble staircase, fine stucco moldings and antiques evoke its illustrious past. But Bellas Artes happily pick-and-mixes contemporary elements with those of the past. The hotel's bedrooms and drawing room have been decorated in a rich palette of royal blue, burgundy, terracotta and sienna which is juxtaposed by walls of plain, dressed stone. Bedrooms are on the small size for a 4 star hotel but the warmth of their decoration and a full quotient of extras are ample compensation. To one side of the patio reception is a cosy drawing room with an honesty bar hidden away inside an antique armoire, a small breakfast room and atop the building a roof terrace from where you can almost reach out and touch those grimacing gargoyles.

To see & do nearby: The sherry bodegas, the Real Escuela de Arte Equestre, visits to Sevilla and Sanlúcar de Barrameda.

CASA VIÑA DE ALCÁNTARA

Antigua Carretera A-38 Jerez - Arcos km 8,6, 11400 Jerez de la Frontera

Tel: 956 393 010 or 650 907 319 Fax: 956 393 011

Email: info@vinadealcantara.com

www.vinadealcantara.com

Management:	Gonzalo del Río y González-Gordon
Closed:	Never
Bedrooms:	5 Doubles and 4 Twins
Prices:	Double/Twin €160 (apart from Horse Fair, Easter a nd Formula 1 weekend) + 7% VAT.
Meals:	Breakfast included, no other meals. There is an excellent restaurant @ 2 minutes drive and Jerez @ 10 minutes.

Directions: From Jerez take A382 towards Arcos de la Frontera. Take first exit, no. 3, for Torremelgarejo/Circuito de Velocidad. Continue on towards Arcos: hotel on right 1km after Hotel Cueva Park.

Cádiz Province · Map 4 · HOTEL 027

If you've stayed at Casa no.7 in Sevilla as a guest of Gonzalo expectations will be high when arriving at his country hotel. You won't be disappointed. The house stands amidst the vineyards of *palomino* grapes that are used to make his family's Tío Pepe *fino*. When the front gates swing open and you see the house's elegant façade of dressed stone the feel is rather like arriving at a Provençal *mas*. A butler will be there to greet you and to carry your suitcases to your bedroom. These bear Gonzalo's distinctive decorative stamp: elegant pastel colour schemes, fine fabrics, antique furniture and top-of-the-range linen, mattresses and bathrooms. Yet the overall feel is more that of a home rather than a hotel and a lovely touch is that his mother's oil paintings are on display throughout the house. There are other works of art and antiques collected by Gonzalo on his travels: they often take him to England which he sees as second home. We walked out at sunset through the exuberant gardens (the swimming pool is fabulous) then on through the vineyards to see water fowl winging across the lake. And then, after a pre-dinner *aperitivo* in the beautiful drawing room, had an exquiste meal at a restaurant just yards from Alcántara. Casa Alcantara would make a blissfully relaxing place to stay for a first or last night in Spain if you're flying in or out of Jerez.

To see & do nearby: Visit to Jerez and the sherry bodegas, the Real Escuela de Arte Equestre and the Grazalema Natural Park.

LA CASA GRANDE

Calle Maldonado 10, 11630 Arcos de la Frontera

Tel: 956 703 930 Fax: 956 717 095

Email: info@lacasagrande.net

www.lacasagrande.net

Management:	Elena Posa
Closed:	January 7 – February 5
Bedrooms:	4 Twin/Doubles, 2 Doubles with private terrace, 1 Junior Suite and 1 Suite
Prices:	Double/Twin €70-81, Double with Terrace €91-97, Junior Suite €81-115, Suite €91-124 + 7% VAT
Meals:	Breakfast €9, light tapas Lunches/Dinners. Several bars and restaurants very close.

Directions: From Jerez A382 towards Arcos. Take first exit for 'Arcos Oeste'. Follow signs Centro Cuidad/Parador. Park in front of Parador. Walk to end of Calle Escribanos, turn right, pass Hotel El Convento, then turn left. Hotel on right.

Cádiz Province · Map 4 · HOTEL 028

There's an art to good living and the Spanish are perhaps the Europeans who live that Epicurean ideal to the fullest. A stay at La Casa Grande as guest of Elena Posa, a fascinating and multilingual *catalana*, is certainly about the better things in life. The position of her house is incredible: this 273-year-old building nudges right up to the very edge of the Arcos cliff. It is a classic seigneurial town house with a grand portal, columned inner patio, huge reception rooms, three floors high. Elena has given the house new life by creating eight guest bedrooms/ suites in its upper floors and in the old cellars. They have been decorated with great panache, happily mixing the original traditional Andalusian features (there are wonderful original floors) with contemporary colours, interesting furnishings and masses of original paintings and drawings. La Casa Grande's breakfast is a feast of orange juice, wonderful bread, local cheeses and first class olive oil, a perfect occasion to try a *tostada con aceite*. But what you will most remember is its rooftop terrace. The views from here are simply beyond belief and when you sit up here at sunset looking south towards the coast, perhaps with a selection of Elena's delicious *tapas*, you'll want to be nowhere else but here.

To see & do nearby: The old town of Arcos, the bodegas and Royal Equestrian School in Jerez, and the villages of the Sierra de Grazalema.

CORTIJO BARRANCO

Ctra Arcos-El Bosque km 5.7, 11630 Arcos de la Frontera

Tel: 956 231 402 Fax: 956 231 209

Email: reservas@cortijobarranco.com

www.cortijobarranco.com

Management:	Genaro Gil Amián
Closed:	Never
Bedrooms:	10 Doubles, 4 Twins and 5 Apartments
Prices:	Double/Twin €57-87, Apartment for 2 €84-119, Apartment for 4 €99-149, Apartment for 6 €129-159 + 7% VAT.
Meals:	Breakfast €4, Lunch/Dinner €25 including wine

Directions: From Jerez A382 to Arcos de la Frontera. Take the third exit, no 29, for Arcos. The road bears right. At roundabout take A372 towards El Bosque. After 5.7 kms, at end of long straight section, turn left at the sign for Barranco (and three flags) then follow a narrow road for 2 kms to the farm.

Barranco, of all the *cortijo* hotels of Andalucía, is perhaps the one that gives you the best feeling for how life on one of these vast country estates was lived. Cutting in from the Arcos road you follow a narrow track that twists up and up for three kilometers, then round a final bend to reach the farm, adrift in a landscape of olives and wheat fields. Massive walls defy the Andalusian sun and crenellated towers remind you that this was once *frontera* country - even if the Moors had long since left Spain when an olive mill was built in 1752. The farm wraps around a classic, arched inner courtyard where you are greeted by the Gil Amián family, or Barranco's resident housekeeper Remedios, before being shown to your room. The leitmotif here is unaffected, old-fashioned comfort: good linen, antique bedsteads with thick mattresses, bright kilims contrasted against the traditional whitewashed walls. There's a comfortable lounge with billiards table and honesty bar and Barranco's breakfasts and candlelit dinners are excellent, served in a beautiful high-ceilinged dining room. Quiet, remote and enchanting, this remains one of my favourite Andalusian hideaways. And horse rides can now be organised out through Barranco's estate: call Remedios for details.

To see & do nearby: Arcos de la Frontera & Medina Sidonia, the Grazalema Park, bodegas & the Royal Equestrian School in Jerez.

HOTEL ARGANTONIO

Calle Argantonio 3, 11004 Cádiz

Tel: 956 211 640 Fax: 956 214 802

Email: reservas@hotelargantonio.com

www.hotelargantonio.com

Management:	Lourdes Martínez
Closed:	Never
Bedrooms:	4 Doubles and 11 Twins
Prices:	Double/Twin €75-95 + 7% VAT
Meals:	Breakfast included, Lunch/Dinner €22-30

Directions: The hotel has reserved (paying) spaces for guests in the Aparcamiento Beato Diego de Cádiz in Calle Beato Diego just beyond the Plaza de las Tortugas on the northern side of the old town. From here it is 2 minute walk to the hotel. See www for exact position of hotel and car park.

Until recently the only decent hotel option in the old centre of Cádiz was the Atlántico, a kind of semi-Parador perched at the ocean's edge. But it is too big, by far, for this guide and just a tad too corporate. So I was delighted to discover this seductive, highly original small hotel during my last visit, just days after it opened for business. Argantonio is tucked away in a quiet pedestrian street at the heart of the old town. The hotel is decorated in *arab-andaluz* style and looks as if it's just been lifted from the Marrakech medina. Everywhere you look are decorative *objets* from the souks: lamps, mirrors, vases and mosaics and, like in the medina, it's all for sale! An intricate horseshoe arch and tiled fountain take pride of place in the central patio and provide the visual focus of the hotel. The oriental theme is carried through to the restaurant and bar whilst the fifteen bedrooms, stacked up on three balustraded floors, vary in decorative style. The best are the top floor rooms which face out to the street: ask for '*una habitación exterior en la planta de arriba*'. But all have been beautifully decorated and have plasma screen TVs, wifi, and sparkling shower rooms. Argantonio's restaurant also looks to the Maghreb, as well as the Med', for inspiration and the food is as appealing as the hotel. Full marks, too, to the bright, attentive staff.

To see & do nearby: The historic centre of Cádiz, boat trips across the bay to El Puerto de Santa María, the Caleta beach, the Santa Catalina museum.

CASA LA LOBA

Calle La Loba 21, 11170 Medina Sidonia

Tel: 956 412 051 or 617 001 176

Email: info@casalaloba.com

www.casalaloba.com

Management:	James Barr
Closed:	Rarely
Bedrooms:	2 Doubles and 1 Suite
Prices:	Double €75-85, Suite €85 including VAT
Meals:	Breakfast included, no other meals. Several lively bars and restaurants very close.

Directions: From Jerez A381 towards Algeciras then exit 24 for Medina Sidonia. Arriving in town follow signs for 'centro urbano' and continue following one way system to the Plazuela de Santiago. Here left into Calle La Loba and house on right after 70 metres.

Cádiz Province · Map 4 · HOTEL 031

Calle La Loba is the jewel in the crown of Medina Sidonia's urban fabric, a long sweep of elegant town houses with some exceptionally fine ironmongery in its ancient *rejas*. James Barr was bowled over by the beauty of the place and next thing found himself the owner of one of its finest houses. That was the easy bit. Next came months of restoration and renovation and the creation of a B&B that could offer the same high standards as the one which James had owned in France. Instead of squeezing in half a dozen rooms he thought big and designed just three: you'll have plenty of space to swing that proverbial cat in both bedrooms and bathrooms. The finish, and level of comfort, is of the best and La Loba is great value compared to places of a similar standard. The decorative philosophy is 'to say a lot with a little' and the house has a clear debt to Zen minimalism. Within the fabric of the house are two patios and in one of them handsome wafer-bricked arches were revealed when the old plaster was being chipped away. At breakfast James will prepare whatever takes your fancy and there's always freshly squeezed orange juice. And be sure to heed James' recommendations on where best to eat. You'll return to Casa Loba having not only eaten very well for very little but probably having made new friends to boot: the unaffected gregariousness of the people of Medina Sidonia is a breath of fresh, *andaluz* air.

To see & do nearby: Medina, Atlantic coast beaches, golf, Vejer, Cádiz, Jerez and the Grazalema sierra.

HOTEL SINDHURA

Patría s/n, La Muela, 11150 Vejer de la Frontera

Tel: 956 448 568/69 Fax: 956 448 550

Email: reservas@hotelsindhura.com

www.hotelsindhura.com

Management:	Ana María García Varra & Alejandro Ortíz de Landaluce
Closed:	December 15 – February 15
Bedrooms:	9 Twins, 3 Doubles, 1 Junior Suite and 1 Suite
Prices:	Double/Twin (terrace) €75-105, Double/Twin (no terrace but sea view) €70-95, Double/Twin (no terrace) €60-85, Junior Suite €95-130, Suite €140-185 + 7% VAT
Meals:	Breakfast included, Lunches weekends only (light snacks available weekdays), Dinner approx. €30

Directions: From Jerez towards Algeciras on A4. Continue past exit for Conil then take the next exit from motorway for La Muela. Follow signs for hotel up hill, past La Muela, to Sindhura.

Cádiz Province · Map 4 · HOTEL 032

Sindhura takes its name from the red-powdered dot or *tilak* that is applied to the forehead of a newlywed bride in India or to that of devotees of Lord Ganesh. Ana and Alejandra's interest in things Eastern runs deep and they chose the lotus as the symbol for their hotel. Their guests come to Sindhura seeking that holy trinity of hostelry: a comfortable room, good food and friendly service. You arrive by way of a track which cuts down towards the sea from Patria, a tiny hamlet just a few kilometers up the hill from Vejer. The building's rather rectilinear form is softened by the palm and olive trees which are getting established and the greenery spills over into its inner patio: in traditional *cortijo* tradition the hotel's focus is inwards as a foil against the summer heat and *levante* wind. Most bedrooms have private terraces and have been tastefully furnished with dark colonial-style tables, desks and chairs, the best being those which face the Atlantic on the first floor. The restaurant also looks outwards and is already reputed for its imaginative salads, excellent cuts of meat and interesting wine list. If you fancy eating out Vejer is just ten minutes back down the road or there's an excellent Italian restaurant just round the corner: you could grab a couple of Sindhura's bikes and cycle there. *Call for details of courses (including Chi Kung).*

To see & do nearby: Beaches in El Palmar and Caños de Meca, day trips to Cádiz, Vejer and Medina Sidonia, walking and cycling in the Sierra de Grazalema.

CASACINCO

Calle Sancho IV El Bravo 5, 11150 Vejer de la Frontera

Tel: 956 455 029 or 626 481301 Fax: 956 451 125

Email: info@hotelcasacinco.com

www.hotelcasacinco.com

Management:	Colette Bardell & Glen Murphy
Closed:	Rarely
Bedrooms:	5 Doubles
Prices:	Double/Twin €80-105 + 7% VAT. Minimum stay 2 nights. Whole house can be rented: email for more information.
Meals:	Breakfast included, no other meals. Masses of restaurants within walking distance.

Directions: From Algeciras E15/N340 north-west towards Cádiz then second turning left for Vejer at km 36. When you reach the town follow signs for Ayuntamiento. When you reach the Plaza de España park car then go through arch at top of square, take the first right and Casa Cinco is on your left.

Cádiz Province · Map 4 · HOTEL 033

Vejer de la Frontera has the unusual credentials of being both a hilltop and coastal town, a sort of Ronda by-the-sea. It's puzzling that it has only recently attracted the attention of northern Europeans in search of their Shangri-La. At the heart of the beautiful old town CasaCinco is one of the most original and intimate places to stay on the Atlantic coast. Stepping in from the street the house seems to wrap you in a warm embrace: you have a real feel of inner sanctum. The ethos of the hotel was inspired by the five senses. Taste is the one you'll remember most: breakfasts are a feast and vary with Colette's mood and the season but will include local cheeses, plenty of fruit, free range eggs and delicious bread. Further sensual pleasure comes in the sounds of great flamenco: music is always present at CasaCinco, bedrooms all have CD players rather than TVs and Glen will offer good advice should you want to buy a few CDs or search out a *peña*. The house's decorative style mixes ethnic and modern and bedrooms have semi-open plan bathrooms. Best of all is CasaCinco's roof terrace which grabs a view of the Atlantic: it is simply magical at night when you can see the lights of Morocco twinkling in the far distance.

To see & do nearby: Whale watching, visits to Jerez bodegas and the Royal Equestrian School, flamenco clubs in Barbate and Vejer.

HOTEL LA CASA DEL CALIFA

Plaza de España 16, 11150 Vejer de la Frontera

Tel: 956 447 730 Fax: 956 451 625

Email: info@lacasadelcalifa.com

www.lacasadelcalifa.com

Management:	Regli Álvarez & James Stuart
Closed:	Never
Bedrooms:	1 Single, 8 Doubles, 7 Twins and 2 Junior Suites
Prices:	Single €50-60, Double/Twin €74-89, Special Double/Twin €97-115, Junior Suite €117-132 + 7% VAT
Meals:	Breakfast included, Lunch/Dinner approx. €30 including wine.

Directions: From Algeciras E15/N340 north-west towards Cádiz then take second turning left for Vejer at km 36. Go up the hill and when you reach the town follow signs for Ayuntamiento. When you reach the Plaza de España the Casa del Califa is on your left.

The history of Andalusia is wrapped within the fabric of La Casa de la Califa's ancient walls. An ancient road - Roman or perhaps even Phoenician - girdles its garden, the Moors chose the spot to build a huge *aljibe*, and the Christians added an enormous grain store. It is said that the Inquisition officiated here and the Nationalists certainly used the place as a barracks in the Civil War. In the most recent chapter of the place's fascinating history the five houses that make up the present building have been converted into a gorgeous small hotel whose fascinating labyrinth of twists, turns, staircases and patios is the complete antithesis of the off-the-peg, chain hotel. Bedrooms are all different in size and configuration, many grab views of Vejer's wonderful roofscape: they are stylish, comfortable and uncluttered. And in a patio-garden which has been sculpted into the rocks at the rear of the building you dine beneath citrus trees on cuisine inspired by the flavours of North Africa: this a fabulous setting for a romantic dinner for two and the wine list reflects James' love of oenology. This seductive, small hotel, like Vejer itself, will soon seduce you with its unique personality.

To see & do nearby: The Natural Park of Los Alcornocales, great beaches at El Palmar and Caños de Meca, visits to the bodegas in Jerez.

TRIPERÍA 1

Tripería 1, 11150 Vejer de la Frontera

Tel: 956 447 730 Fax: 956 451 625

Email: triperia@vejer.com

www.vejer.com/triperia

Management:	Regli Álvarez & James Stuart
Closed:	Never
Bedrooms:	3 Twin/Doubles, 2 Junior Suites and 1 Family Room
Prices:	Double/Twin €72-108 , Junior Suite €88-125, Family Room €130-163 + 7% VAT
Meals:	Breakfast approx. €7.50 next door at La Casa del Califa or in square.

Directions: From Algeciras E15/N340 north-west towards Cádiz then take second turning left for Vejer at km 36. Go up the hill then follow signs for Ayuntamiento. When you reach the Plaza de España collect keys from the Casa del Califa, on left of square.

Cádiz Province · Map 4 · HOTEL 035

The latest acquisition of Regli and James is just yards from their fabulous Casa del Califa hotel and just to one side of the pretty Plaza de España. This is one of those Andalusian houses that gives little away from the outside. Passing through an unassuming entrance things open out into a large patio where there is a huge pool surrounded by potted plants with fabulous views across the rooftops to the pine forests of Montenmedio and to the Natural Park of Las Marismas. Tripería's bedrooms are enormous and have top spec bathrooms, beds and fittings and each has its own terrace. They are spotlessly clean and Moroccan artefacts and contemporary works of art add a dash of decorative razzmatazz: the overall feel is more homely than hotel-like. You can eat breakfast at Tripería but it would be much nicer to eat next door in Califa's leafy courtyard or at one of the little cafés in the square, a great spot to while away a few hours with your book or just watching the world go by. When it comes to planning your sorties James is your man. He has lived for two decades in this delectable town, runs his own travel agency, writes for local magazines and has a deep knowledge of Andalusian culture from food to wine to flamenco.

To see & do nearby: Atlantic coast beaches, day trips to Cádiz and Jerez and walking in nearby parks of Grazalema & Los Alcornocales.

ESCONDRIJO

Callejón Oscuro 3, 11150 Vejer de la Frontera

Tel: 956 447 438 or 669 950 305

Email: info@escondrijo.com

www.escondrijo.com

Management:	Netty Ludlow & Nigel Anderson
Closed:	Mid November – end February
Bedrooms:	1 Double and 4 Suites
Prices:	Double €85-100, Suite €95-135 + 7% VAT
Meals:	Breakfast included

Directions: From Algeciras N340 north-west towards Cádiz then take second turning left for Vejer at km 36. Go up the hill and when you reach the town follow signs for Ayuntamiento. When you reach the Plaza de España park car then go through arch at top of square, up hill to the Vera Cruz restaurant and here go left: Escondrijo on left.

Cádiz Province · Map 4 · HOTEL 036

Escondrijo is well-named: literally it means 'the hideaway' and this delectable B&B is tucked away in a narrow pedestrian street in Vejer's old town. The place has a fascinating history, once forming part of a much larger house which was built on the site of a chapel destroyed in the 1755 earthquake (remember reading Voltaire's *Candide*?). Netty and Nigel, young professionals on the run from London, came here with the brief of creating an original, supremely comfortable boutique B&B that would live up to the Spanish dictum *nuestra casa es vuestra casa*. The four suites are really spacious with a great mix of old and new: wafer-bricking, terracotta floor tiles, interesting art, both period and contemporary, and great bathrooms. The two on the top floor have private terraces with loungers. Downstairs in the flagged inner courtyard is a corner bar with some great wines and, to one side, an internet corner and cosy lounge with piles of books. Breakfast is served here around one huge square table and is a brunch-style feast: freshly squeezed orange juice, ham, cheese and eggs, homemade granola, and excellent coffee. And Escondrijo's rooftop terrace is a great spot to unwind: it has sun loungers and soaring views out across the rooftops of Vejer. *Hotel will be closed due to building works until June 2008.*

To see & do nearby: Contemporay art exhibitions at the NMAC, day trips to Cádiz, riding, the beach at El Palmar.

HOTEL LA BREÑA

Avenida de Trafalgar 1, 11160 Los Caños de Meca

Tel: 956 437 368 or 627 424 343 Fax: 956 437 368

Email: info@hotelbrena.com

www.hotelbrena.com

Management:	José Mañuel Morillo Doncel-Moriano
Closed:	End October – March
Bedrooms:	4 Twins and 3 Junior Suites.
Prices:	Twin/Junior Suite €55-115 including VAT
Meals:	Breakfast €5, Lunch/Dinner approx. €25 including wine

Directions: From Algeciras N340/E15 towards Cádiz/Sevilla to Vejer de la Frontera. Continue past town then turn left and follow signs to Caños de Meca. Here continue straight through village towards Barbate. Hotel is at very end of village on left, signposted.

Caños de Meca's fabulous beaches have long been popular with *gaditanos* out-on-the-weekend as well as with a colourful band of travellers from further afield who come here in search of a Goa closer to home. Just yards from its best stretch of sand La Breña is a young, lighthearted hotel which seems to mirror its owners' friendly, outgoing nature. The place's best feature is the front dining terrace which looks out to the Atlantic: lunch or dinner can't fail to be a special occasion. And where better to try the local speciality, *atún de almadraba*, the most famous export of neighbouring Barbate? If you dine inside the feel-good factor is still right up the scale: restaurant and bar area have a stylish commingling of designerish furniture and modern art (the exhibited works changing from time to time) with masses of light slanting in from the sea-facing terrace. And the bedrooms are great value considering that you're just yards from the sand. All are enormous, with bathrooms to match, cleaned to pristine perfection by Breña's friendly staff, and with the same *chic*, uncluttered lines as the restaurant. I'd choose an attic room with a terrace but all of them are really great. And José Mañuel makes every one of his visitors feel like an honoured guest.

To see & do nearby: Unspoilt beaches, Vejer de la Frontera, the Roman ruins at Bolonia.

HOTEL MADRESELVA

Avenida de Trafalgar 102, 11159 Los Caños de Meca

Tel: 956 437 255 Fax: 956 437 066

Email: madreselvahotel@cherrytel.com

www.madreselvahotel.com

....

Management:	José Ramón Vázquez
Closed:	November – Easter
Bedrooms:	12 Doubles, 6 Twins and 1 Suite
Prices:	Double/Twin €57-78, Suite €110-139 including VAT
Meals:	Buffet breakfast included, no other meals but several good bars and restaurants in vicinity.

....

Directions: From Algeciras N340/E15 towards Cádiz/Sevilla to Vejer de la Frontera. Continue past town then turn left and follow signs to Caños de Meca. Here continue straight through village along beach in direction of Barbate, pass chemist and you'll see Hotel Madreselva to the left.

Caños sees a lot of action during the summer months when Spaniards and the international surfing community head for the beach. Out of season it has a very different feel and is a great place to kick back, walk in the Natural Park of La Breña and chill out on some of the Atlantic coast's finest beaches. Madreselva is a stone's throw from the sea and this clean, laid-back and attractive small hotel is one of the best places to stay in the area. The bar-cum-breakfast room has a bright, fresh feel about it and the bedrooms are in the same vein: crisp white bedspreads, good linen, and with interesting contemporary paintings adding a dash of colour. All rooms have their own terraces which horseshoe round the central, plant-filled patio and there's a large swimming pool just beyond. Breakfast at Madreselva is a buffet-style feast and, although no other meals are served, there's a great fish retaurant a few hundred metres along the beach as well as a funky, beachside bar - a perfect place for sundowners. From here there is a beautiful cliffside path which you can follow all the way to neighbouring Barbate, Cape Trafalgar is on your doorstep, so too are some great beaches (nudist in parts) and wonderful Vejer is just a hop away.

To see & do nearby: Beaches and watersports, golf at Montenmedio, riding and walking in the coastal Park.

LA HORMIGA VOLADORA

El Lentiscal 18, 11391 Bolonia – Tarifa

Tel: 956 688 562 Fax: 956 688 562

Management:	Julia Muñoz Fernández & Rafael Chico Jiménez
Closed:	Never
Bedrooms:	9 Doubles, 4 Twins and 3 Apartments
Prices:	Double/Twin €50-60, Apartment €70-80 including VAT
Meals:	Breakfasts (only served from 15 July– 15 September) approx. €5.

Directions: From Algeciras head north on the E15/N340 towards Cádiz. Pass Tarifa and at km 70 turn left at signs for Bolonia. As you arrive in the village turn left at the Bella Vista Hostal. The road soon bears hard to the left. Hormiga Voladora is on the right after 100 metres.

If you ask most folk who know Andalusia's Atlantic coast which is their favourite beach you can be fairly certain what the answer will be: Bolonia. Not only does it have a beautiful arc of sand and dunes and some great fish restaurants but also, just yards from the beach, are the Roman ruins of Baelo Claudio: two thousand years ago the garum paste that was made here ended up on the very best tables in Rome. There are a couple of bog-standard *hostals* and masses of dull apartments in the village but by far the nicest place to stay is La Hormiga Voladora. This simple little hostelry is right next to the sea, surrounded by a thick stand of bamboo: if you've ever been here when the *levante* wind has been blowing you'll understand why it isn't cut down to open up views of the sea. The hostal's bedrooms are simple, rather Spartan in feel, but perfectly adequate considering their low price tag. Some have their own bathrooms, others have small shower rooms which are reached by crossing a small courtyard. Breakfasts, in season, are served in a pretty patio beneath a huge mulberry tree and Rafael and Julia, the friendly owners, can recommend where to eat the best fish in the village.

To see & do nearby: Whale and dolphin-watching excursions, the Roman ruins of Baelo Claudio, day trips to Morocco.

HOTEL PUNTA SUR

Ctra Cádiz-Málaga km 77, 11380 Tarifa

Tel: 956 684 326 Fax: 956 680 472
Email: hotelpuntasur@cherrytel.com
www.hotelpuntasur.com

Management:	Juan Antonio Nuñez
Closed:	Occasionally in winter – check!
Bedrooms:	16 Doubles, 6 Twins, 6 Suites and 4 Family Bungalows
Prices:	Double/Twin €83-155, Family Room €153-220, Suite €163-230 + 7% VAT
Meals:	Breakfast included, Lunch approx. €25, Dinner approx. €30 including wine.

Directions: From Cádiz take the N340/E15 south towards Algeciras. Hotel Punta Sur is to the left of the N340/E15 close to km post 77.

James Whaley is a master in the art of transforming hotels and hostels which seem destined to remain commonplace into some of the most innovative, stylish and spicey places to stay on the Atlantic coast. He had a fantastic site and gardens when he turned his hand to Punta Sur, and since he took over the bungalow-style rooms have seen complete metamorphosis. He didn't limit himself to the nearest *Ikea* when it came to decoration but instead headed for North Africa, the States, even Indonesia, in search of floors, prints, lamps and photographs. Each bedroom has been decorated to evoke a different place in the world including Bali, Java, Cuba, Congo and Miami. All of the rooms have private terraces which look across a sweep of lawn that runs up to the massive swimming pool. The restaurant and bar area's decoration is fabulous: this is a light and airy space with glass and slightly Gaudí-esque ceramic murals and interesting modern art adding a big twist of style. The food, too, mixes the best of local culinary tradition with dishes from further afield. Vegetables, meat and fish are all brought in fresh from the local market.

To see & do nearby: Roman ruins of Baelo Claudio, the Estrecho de Gibraltar and Los Alcornocales Parks, kite and windsurfing along the Tarifa coast.

HOTEL HURRICANE

Ctra de Málaga a Cádiz km 78, 11380 Tarifa

Tel: 956 684 919 Fax: 956 680 329

Email: info@hurricanehotel.com

www.hurricanehotel.com

Management:	James Whaley
Closed:	Never
Bedrooms:	35 Doubles, Twins and Suites
Prices:	Sea-facing Double/Twin €100-155, Mountain facing Double/Twin €83-140, Family Suite €141-227, Luxury Suite €171-266 + 7% VAT
Meals:	Breakfast €9, Lunch €15, Dinner €30 including wine

Directions: From Cádiz take the N340/E15 south. Hurricane Hotel is to the right of the N340/E15 approx. 7 kms before you reach Tarifa. Signposted.

Cádiz Province · Map 4 · HOTEL 041

The Hurricane owes its existence to James and Belinda Whaley who saw in a simple roadside *hostal* a vision of better things to come. In the early years most guests were from the windsurfing community but nowadays the clientele are much more diverse. They choose to stay here for the simple pleasure of staying just yards from the mighty breakers of the Atlantic and the unique feel of the Hurricane: laid-back, spicey...different. There are fabulous gardens, two pools, a gym, stables, kitesurfing school and a terrace bar which looks straight out across the waves to the Rif. The best rooms, of course, are those with sea views but all are stylish in an understated way with a sculptural/decorative debt to things Moroccan (James used to own the Villa Maroc in Essaouira). The Hurricane's food is a great mix of Spanish and International, the lunchtime buffet excellent and vegetarians get a great choice of dishes. And there's always plenty of fresh fish on the menu. But when the place really comes into its own is at night when you dine beneath the stars in the candlelit garden surrounded by the Hurricane's luxuriant greenery. This is a perfect place for a romantic break but you'll need to book months ahead if you're planning to come in season.

To see & do nearby: Roman ruins of Baelo Claudio, Natural Parks of Estrecho de Gibraltar and Los Alcornocales, the Atlantic coast beaches.

EL ESCONDITE DEL VIENTO

Calle Comendador 1, 11380 Tarifa

Tel: 956 681 901 Fax: 956 682 771
Email: contacto@elesconditedelviento.com
www.elesconditedelviento.com

Management:	Alejandra Pablos & José Mateos
Closed:	Mid January – mid February
Bedrooms:	6 Twin/Doubles and 1 Triple
Prices:	Smaller Double €90-125, Double/Twin with balcony €100-135, Double/Twin with terrace €110-145, Triple €125-160 + 7% VAT
Meals:	Breakfast included, Dinner approx. €30

Directions: From Algeciras N340/E15 towards Cádiz then take first exit for Tarifa. Follow signs to port and leave car at car park just inside of port gates. From here it is just a two minute walk to the hotel which is at the heart of the old town of Tarifa: see www for exact position of hotel.

Cádiz Province · Map 4 · HOTEL 042

Tarifa has witnesed an extraordinary metamorphosis over the past decade: think 'hip' and 'Atlantic Coast', think Tarifa. In amongst its plethora of chic boutiques, sushi bars and surf-gear shops is a hotel with as much designer attitude as the town itself. Escondite turns its back on that samey *andaluz rústico* style in favour of the contemporary and the innovative. Alejandra and José were the alchemists, drawing on years of world travel when conceptualising their hotel. They oversaw the makeover of an 18th century town house, marrying steel, wood and glass in an inspirational series of spaces which double as a showcase for 20th century design classics: Sarrinen's Tulip chair, van der Rohe's Barcelona bed, Nelson's marshmallow armchair. Every corner of the hotel was created for maximum visual and aesthetic effect and the result is both serene and uplifting. The bedrooms are fabulous: they have funky fans, flat-screen TVs, lights that turn on and off with a wave of a hand, slick taps and door handles, crisp linen sheets and a seamless blend of slate, smoked glass, stone with bright splashes of colours. The restaurant is just as slick: breakfast late, dine on innovative Mediterranean cuisine and relax into one of the few hotels in Andalucía to have truly embraced the Noughties.

To see & do nearby: Day trips to Morocco, the beaches of the Atlantic Coast, whale and dolphin watching, the old town of Tarifa.

CASA CONVENTO LA ALMORAIMA

Ctra Algeciras-Ronda, 11350 Castellar de la Frontera

Tel: 956 693 002 Fax: 956 693 214

Email: casaconventoalmoraima@telefonica.net

www.la-almoraima.com

Management:	Lidia Espinosa
Closed:	Never
Bedrooms:	3 Singles, 1 Double and 13 Twins
Prices:	Single €63, Double/Twin €99 including VAT
Meals:	Breakfast €8, Lunch/Dinner €20 including wine

Directions: From Marbella take the AP7/E15 towards Algeciras then branch onto A369 towards Jimena de la Frontera. La Almoraima is signposted to the left, close to the turning for Castellar de la Frontera.

Almoraima has a colourful history. It was built by the Duke of Medinacelli who later rented it to an order of monks. The family had second thoughts - you'll understand why should you visit the place - so they grabbed it back for use as a private hunting lodge. Sacked by Napoleon's troops, the Medinacelli family eventually sold it to a bank. Finally it was expropriated by the state and turned into one of Andalucía's most seductive country hotels. If Almoraima's balustraded façade and Florentine belfry make for a grand *entrée*, once you enter the cloistered patio you are enveloped in a magical and intimate world-within-world where plants, birdsong and the scent of orange blossom are conducive to blissful relaxation. Bedrooms are sober and comfortable, there's an elegant lounge with an honesty bar and Andalusian cuisine - simple rather than gourmet - served in a chandeliered dining room. And you won't want for space: the monastery is surrounded by 16,000 hectares of estate which is yours to explore on foot, on horseback or in a 4x4. Be sure to drive up to nearby Castellar de la Frontera, one of Andalucía's most spectacular hill villages and home to a colourful community of hippy incomers.

To see & do nearby: Visits to Castellar de la Fontera and the Natural Park of Los Alcornocales, day trips to Gibraltar and Morocco.

HOTEL MONASTERIO DE SAN MARTÍN

Ctra Comarcal CA-513 km 4, Montegral Alto
11340 San Martín del Tesorillo

Tel: 956 618 515/725 Fax: 956 618 691
Email: info@hotelmonasteriodesanmartin.com
www.hotelmonasteriodesanmartin.com

Management:	Lina Rodríguez
Closed:	In winter: check with hotel for exact dates
Bedrooms:	16 Doubles, 1 Superior Double and 4 Suites
Prices:	Double €115-140, Superior Double €125-150, Suite €150-175 + 7% VAT. Prices approximate!
Meals:	Breakfast €15, Lunch/Dinner from €35 excluding drinks

Directions: From Estepona AP7 (peaje/toll road) towards Algeciras. Exit for exit at km 133 for Torreguadiaro then follow signs to San Martín del Tesorillo. Here continue through village towards Gaucín. Hotel is signposted to right after approx. 4 kms.

Cádiz Province · Map 5 · HOTEL 044

The idea of building a new hotel in the style of a 17th century monastery is, it must be said, unusual. But so too are most good ideas and if you book a night at San Martín you'll be in for a big treat. The hotel is only a couple of years old but you'd guess that it had been around for much longer: the enormous pines and ancient olives that were transplanted and the lawns and bougainvillaea are fast rooting down. Fabulous old wooden doors lead through to an airy reception area and the high-ceilinged restaurant whose menu looks to the best of Andalucía's traditional cuisine. Across the way is a large guest lounge where there are gilded mirrors, repro prints of English hunting scenes, antique dressers, masses of sofas and a rather lonesome looking grand piano. But the architectural highlight is the arched cloister, graced with four high palms, citrus trees, a central fountain, and where there are shaded terraces with wicker chairs as well as bright, Moroccan-tiled tables. San Martin's bedrooms all give onto this exquisite central patio and are deeply comfortable, decorated with immense razzle-dazzle and have all the extras that you'd expect of a four star hotel. So leave the hair shirt at home and arrive safe in the knowledge that you're getting a lot of comfort for your euros.

To see & do nearby: Beaches on both Mediterranean and Atlantic coasts, Gaucín and the white villages, Gibraltar and day trips to Morocco.

HOSTAL EL ANÓN

Calle Consuelo 34-40, 11330 Jimena de la Frontera

Tel: 956 640 113 or 956 640 416 Fax: 956 641 110

Email: reservas@elanon.net

www.hostalanon.com

Management:	Suzanna Odell & Gabriel Delgado
Closed:	2 weeks end June, 2 weeks end November
Bedrooms:	2 Singles, 5 Twins, 2 Triples, 2 Quadruples and 1 Apartment
Prices:	Single €42, Double/Twin €65, Triple €95, Quadruple €120, Apartment €75 including VAT
Meals:	Breakfast included, Lunch/Dinner approx. €25 including wine. Bar snacks also available. Restaurant & bar closed on Wednesdays.

Directions: From Málaga AP7 west towards Algeciras. Exit for Sotogrande/Castellar. Through Valderrama, cross railway bridge, then turn right on the A369 to Jimena. Head up through village then turn left and follow signs to El Anon.

Suzanna Odell has lived in Jimena for many years and opened El Anon long before the hilltop villages of this part of Spain became known by the expat community. A number of village houses were gradually wrapped into the fabric of her *hostal*, creating an intimate, organic and delightfully rambling place to stay. Each of the bedrooms is different to the next. Some give onto inner patio-courtyards, others to the village's whitewashed streets, making some of them light, others rather darker. The emphasis is on simple, rustic, uncluttered comfort rather than on gadgetry and four-star finery. You can see why El Anon's rooms appeal to walkers and the place is popular with groups from the UK who use it as a base from which to explore the footpaths through the Alcornocales Natural Park. The restaurant and bar feel as cosy as the rest of the hotel, breakfasts include home-made bread and fresh orange juice and the lunch and dinner menu looks to Spain and Morocco for its inspiration. The staff are young and friendly and the whole place is imbued by Suzanna's relaxed and friendly nature. If you enjoy walking get hold of a copy of my book *Walking in Andalucía* which lists two beautiful circuits leading straight out from Jimena.

To see & do nearby: Jimena's castle, walks along the Hozgarganta river valley, the cave paintings of Laja Alta.

HOTEL JIMENA REAL

Calle Sevilla 44, 11330 Jimena de la Frontera

Tel: 956 648 130 Fax: 956 648 144

Email: info@jimenarealhotel.com

www.jimenarealhotel.com

Management:	Robert Noonan
Closed:	Occasionally in winter: check!
Bedrooms:	3 Doubles, 6 Twins and 4 Suites
Prices:	Double/Twin €95-115, Suite €125-145 + 7% VAT. Prices approximate!
Meals:	Breakfast €10, no Lunch/Dinner but several lively bars and restaurants very close to hotel.

Directions: From Málaga AP7 west towards Algeciras. Exit for Sotogrande/Castellar. Through Valderrama, cross railway bridge, then turn right on the A369 to Jimena. Follow main street, Calle Sevilla, through village. Hotel is on right shortly before you reach the flags of the 'Ayuntamiento' (town hall).

Jimena is expanding fast at the periphery yet its old centre retains oodles of charm. The village has some of the best *tapas* bars in the province and the walks here, along the beautiful Hozgaraganta river valley and up and into the park, are amongst my favourites in Andalucía: see my book *Walking in Andalucía*. Jimena Real is the first hotel in the village to place the accent firmly on luxury and its creators have fashioned an exceptionally attractive series of spaces within the carapace of this ancient village house. The hotel is built around a splendid triple-tiered, balustraded courtyard, topped by a glass atrium which brings in masses of light. Huge mirrors enhance the effect, enormous leather sofas and arm chairs to either side of the entrance promise deep comfort and throughout the hotel intricate mosaic work (created by Casa Mosaico in Gaucín: see their entry in this book) embellishes and beautifies. The basement dining room and bar, and its terrace, look north to the Hacha mountain and several bedrooms grab that same view. They have bright colour washes, top of the range bedding and bathrooms that can't be faulted. The only downside is that the reception is left unattended during the middle part of the day so be sure to let the hotel know your E.T.A..

To see & do nearby: Walking in the Natural Park of Los Alcornocales, day trips to Gibraltar and to Morocco, the Roman ruins at Bolonia.

LA MEJORANA

Calle Santa Clara 6, 11610 Grazalema

Tel: 956 132 327 or 649 613 272

Email: info@lamejorana.net

www.lamejorana.net

Management:	Ana Vázquez & Andrés Sánchez
Closed:	July & August
Bedrooms:	4 Doubles and 1 Twin
Prices:	Double/Twin €55-60 including VAT
Meals:	Breakfast included, no other meals. Several restaurants just yards away.

Directions: From Ronda A374 towards Sevilla then left to Grazalema. Here in the main square turn sharp right and head up the street to the left of the Unicaja bank. Turn right at small fountain into Calle Pontezuela. La Mejorana signposted at end of street.

Grazalema is the best known of the *pueblos blancos*, a string of whitewashed mountain villages that stretches from Arcos to Ronda. It attracts increasing numbers of visitors and at the weekends the village struggles to keep its feet when Spaniards from Cádiz and Sevilla head for the hills. During the week it remains a sleepy mountain village and is a great base if you're planning to walk in the Grazalema National Park. The nicest place to stay is La Mejorana, tucked well away from the main drag in a quiet cul-de-sac. Unusual for a village house, it has a large garden and pool and its lofty position means that you get great views out to the rocky hillsides which cradle the village. Ana and Andrés, the friendly young owners, have decorated the house with the family's antiques and contemporary works of art. The feel is really homely and light floods in to the drawing room and breakfast gallery from its many windows. The best bedrooms are those that catch the view but all are warm, quiet and comfortable. The garden has a number of inviting shaded areas amongst the roses, olives and palms, just perfect for relaxing after a day of walking in the hills. But it's a shame that the included breakfast is uninspiring: I'd rather head down to the square and have decent coffee, orange juice and *tostadas* with the locals.

To see & do nearby: Walking and riding in the Grazalema Natural Park, ornithological excurions, visit to the blanket factory and its museum mill.

HOTELS 048 – 097

MÁLAGA

CORTIJO EL PAPUDO

11340 San Martín del Tesorillo

Tel: 952 854 018 or 617 244 392 Fax: 952 854 018

Email: papudo@mercuryin.es

www.andalucia.com/gardens/papudo

Management:	Vivien & Michael Harvey
Closed:	Never
Bedrooms:	4 Doubles and 7 Twins
Prices:	Double/Twin €70 including VAT
Meals:	Breakfast included, no other meals. Simple restaurants in village just a short drive from farm.

Directions: From Estepona AP7 (peaje/toll road) towards Algeciras. Exit at km 133 for San Martín del Tesorillo then follow signs for San Martín del Tesorillo. Here, arriving in village, just before reaching the river, turn right. Continue for 1.5 kms. 150 metres after you begin to climb first hill sharp left into the drive of El Papudo. Signposted.

Málaga Province · Map 5 · HOTEL 048

The small village of San Martín lies at the southern end of the Guadiaro valley, just a few miles inland from Sotogrande. The exceptionally mild, moist climate of this part of Andalucía means that subtropical species thrive and the village is surrounded by vast plantations of fruit trees. This fecund climate also explains the existence of a number of garden centres. The Harveys own one of the best of them and they recently restored and renovated the neighbouring *cortijo* to create a small country B&B. The gardens, as you'd expect, are fantastic and anyone with even a passing interest in things horticultural will love the symphony of colour and texture that Vivien and Michael have created from plants, trees and shrubs. It teems with birdlife and there's a pretty pool sculpted into the greenery, heated at either end of the season. When converting the old granary to create the bedrooms they tried to change as little as possible. Original beams and tiles are still in place and the abundance of wood gives the simple bedrooms a welcoming feel. This could be a great choice if you're looking for a quiet place to unwind - it would be blissful to sit and read in the cobbled patio - and there are good restaurants a short drive away. A great mid-range choice is La Cabaña in Soto Grande or, cheap and cheerful, Mesón Amanecer is just along the road in San Martín.

To see & do nearby: The fortified hill town of Castellar de la Frontera, dolphin watching out from La Linea or Gibraltar, beaches and birdwatching.

HOTEL HACIENDA LA HERRIZA

Ctra Gaucín - El Colmenar km 6, 29480 Gaucín

Tel: 951 068 200 Fax: 951 068 219
Email: info@laherriza.com
www.laherriza.com

Management:	Antonio Rodríguez Álvarez & David Oliver Rodríguez
Closed:	December 24 & 25, January 8-February 9
Bedrooms:	17 Junior Suites sleeping 2 or 4
Prices:	House for 2 €99-119, House for 4 €179-215 + 7% VAT. Special offers available throughout the year.
Meals:	Breakfast included, Lunch/Dinner €29-40 including wine

Directions: From Marbella A7/E15 then AP7 toll motorway towards Cádiz then take exit 142 for Gaucín/Casares then A377 to Casares then on to Gaucín. Here left at junction then left again at petrol station on A405 towards Algeciras. After 2 kms turn right at sign for El Colmenar. Hotel is on right after 4.5 kms.

La Herriza is hidden away in the forests that lie between Gaucín and its tiny railway station, El Colmenar. This is a place for folk who like to get well off the beaten track and the individual houses that make up this complex are ideal if you really value your intimacy. There are seventeen of them and all have been designed and decorated with a maximum of comfort in mind. They have phones, TVs and wifi, and carved Ronda-style furniture which is nicely complemented by warm colour washes, coco matting and pretty stencilling. Restaurant, bar, reception, and a huge upstairs drawing room are in an adjacent building where huge glass windows bring in the light and a wonderful view out across the surrounding cork oaks and almond groves. And the food here is amongst the best in the area. 'Gourmet, Mediterranean Fusion' is how the management like to describe it but there are some more traditional dishes, too, and the menu constantly changes following the dictates of the season. And there's a wine list to match the food with a choice of no less than 250 different bottles. This could be an excellent base for a walking holiday or, if you prefer two wheels, guests have free use of the hotel's mountain bikes.

To see & do nearby: The Colmenar gorge, the valley of the river Genal and Ronda and the white villages.

LA ALMUÑA

Apartado de Correos 20, 29480 Gaucín

Tel: 952 151 200 Fax: 952 151 343

Email: laalmuna@telefonica.net

www.gaucin.com

Management:	Diana Paget
Closed:	Never
Bedrooms:	2 Singles, 4 Doubles, 2 Twins and 1 Apartment for 4
Prices:	Single €60, Double/Twin €120, Cottage for 4 people €900 per week + 7% VAT
Meals:	Breakfast included, Dinner €30 including wine

Directions: From Estepona AP7 (peaje/toll road) towards Algeciras. Take exit 142 for Casares/Gaucín. Arriving in Gaucín turn left at first junction then left again at petrol station on A405 towards Algeciras. At km 44.8 turn left at round post into 'La Almuña' estate. Diana's is the house to right of track behind a line of cypress trees.

Málaga Province · Map 5 · HOTEL 050

There is nowhere to stay in Spain quite like La Almuña, one of the few B&Bs which really does live up to the Spanish dictum of *mi casa es tu casa* – my home is your home. This laid-back B&B is within the original farmhouse on a large estate which is now shared by a number of (mostly British) families. The life and soul of the place is Diana Paget. Hers is a relaxed, shambolic and utterly welcoming home of the take-us-as-you-find-us type. Swallows nest in the kitchen, dogs lounge on the sofas, friends pop in and out for a cup of tea or a gin and tonic whilst Diana carrys on unperturbed with her culinary preparations, the antithesis of the Forté manager. And her dinners are always special with an easy flow of food and wine: guests staying at neighbouring houses will often join in the feast. From here there are incredible views out over the rolling farmlands south of Gaucín to the distant Moroccan Rif. Although parts of the house are getting a little worn at the edges, guests return year after year to stay with Diana, some to walk, some to ride, others just to chill out in the best of company. I, for one, always really look forward to my stays at La Almuña.

To see & do nearby: Walking and riding in the Gaucín area, the train ride north to Ronda, the Tarifa beaches, the Roman ruins at Bolonia.

LA FRUCTUOSA

Calle Convento 67, 29480 Gaucín

Tel: 617 692 784 Fax: 952 151 580
Email: lafructuosa@yahoo.es
www.lafructuosa.com

Management:	Luis Ruibérriz & Jesús Balsa
Closed:	Never
Bedrooms:	3 Doubles, 2 Twins and 1 house sleeping up to 4
Prices:	Double/Twin €88-98, House €440-880 including VAT
Meals:	Breakfast included, Dinner €30-35 including wine.
	Restaurant open Easter-November on Fridays & Saturdays.

Directions: From Estepona AP7 (peaje/toll road) towards Algeciras. Take exit 142 for Casares/Gaucín. Arrving in Gaucín turn right at T junction and follow this street into the village. La Fructuosa is on the right just before you come to a small square and a 'farmacía'.

La Fructuosa is plumb in the centre of the pretty, hilltop village of Gaucín and grabs a magnificent view southwards to Gibraltar and, beyond, the Moroccan Rif mountains. Luis and Jesús are easy, cosmopolitan hosts who have shown enormous sensitivity in the restoration of this former *lagar*, preserving whatever they could of the original building whilst introducing bold colours (made with natural pigments brought from as far afield as Egypt and Tunisia) and modern decorative elements. There are five bedrooms and a guest lounge on the top two floors whose decoration was a labour of decorative love. There are handmade ceramic tiles and polished stucco in the bathrooms, ragged and sponged paint finishes, cut flowers, rugs from Tunisia and Afghanistan. The basement restaurant doubles as a gallery for local artists. Its cuisine looks to the Med' for inspiration and to the season for its ingredients: the only down side is that it's not open more often! Stay here and you'll bless the day your hosts' car broke down and they were forced to make an unscheduled stop in Gaucín, eventually deciding to stay for good. The hotel has excellent route notes for a number of walks in the area.

To see & do nearby: Walking in the Gaucín area, day trip to Tangier, visits to Ronda and the white villages, the Atlantic coast beaches.

CASA MOSAICO

Calle Portichuelo 53, 29480 Gaucín

Tel: 952 151 448 or 600 785 445 Fax: 952 151 580

Email: emma@realmosaic.com

www.realmosaic.com

Management:	Emma Cornish & Stephen Windsor-Clive
Closed:	Never
Bedrooms:	1 Twin, 1 Double and 1 Casita
Prices:	Twin €110 , Double €130, Casita €200 or €800 per week inc. VAT. 10% discount for non-bridge players & agnostics
Meals:	Breakfast included, Lunch/Dinner €40 including wine, by prior arrangement.

Directions: From Estepona AP7 (peaje/toll road) towards Algeciras. Take exit 142 for Casares/Gaucín. Arriving in Gaucín turn left then at petrol station turn right towards Ronda. Go round 2 bends, cross bridge then right up a steep concrete ramp into the village. House is on left at the top hill.

Emma and Stephen's Andalusian retreat is, as the name suggests, an ode to the art of mosaic. He is an expert in the field having studied in Ravenna and London and then set up his own workshop in Morocco. Nearly every corner of this enormous Gaucín house – floors, tables, murals, and decorative *objets* – has been embellished and beautified with their unique *tessarai* design and artistry. At Casa Mosaico you choose between a room in the main house – they have coir-matted or mosaic floors, Moroccan rugs, first class linen and funky bathrooms – or the *casita* which has its own palm-shaded terrace, galley kitchen, lounge, bedroom and chill-out roof terrace. All of it has been decorated in *arab-andaluz* style with a big twist of razzmatazz. The terraces and gardens take on another dimension at night when candles and Moroccan appliqué lighting add further zing to the Eastern theme. And if you join your hosts for dinner you're guaranteed a memorable evening. Emma's dinners look to the Mediterranean for inspiration and if you've been travelling for a while in Andalucía you'll appreciate the high veggie quotient. Stephen will happily organise a day trip to Morocco with his trusted local guides. *For more information on mosaics and courses see www.realmosaic.com.*

To see & do nearby: Day trips to Morocco, walking in the Alcornocales Park, beaches on both the Mediterranean and Atlantic coasts.

EL NOBO

Apartado de Correos 46, 29480 Gaucín

Tel: 952 151 303 or 680 453 899 Fax: 952 117 207
Email: elnobo@terra.es
www.elnobo.co.uk

Management:	Sally & Christopher Von Meister
Closed:	July & August
Bedrooms:	2 Doubles, 1 Master Suite, 1 Cottage and 1 Villa sleeping 4
Prices:	Double €130, Master Suite €150 including VAT. Prices for Villa/Cottage on request.
Meals:	Breakfast included, Dinner €37 inc. wine, by prior arrangement.

Directions: From Estepona AP7 towards Algeciras. Take exit 142 for Casares/Gaucín. Arriving in Gaucín right at T junction then continue past La Fructuosa to a small square. Here turn sharp right at sign 'Camino de Gibraltar'. Follow track downhill for 800m: house on left.

You'll need to travel a long way to find as magnificent a setting as this. El Nobo straddles a hilltop just beneath Gaucín with views that defy description. Be here at sunset and you'll understand why this is one of the most photographed houses in Andalucía. Sally and Christopher told me that the most common reaction of new-arrivals when faced with the view down to Gibraltar and to the mountains of North Africa is simply an awe-inspired 'wow!'. The interior design and décor gets all the journalists purring: Condé Nast, the Sunday Times, and Spanish style mag Casa y Campo have all waxed lyrical about the country-style furnishings, beautiful colour schemes and the stunning garden that has been sculpted amongst the natural rock. Breakfast is a generous affair, dinners are candlelit and fabulous and it's hard to pull yourself away from El Nobo's beautiful terrace. Both the villa and cottage would be perfect if you're looking for a romantic, hidden, luxurious retreat and there are great walks straight out from the house (see my book *Walking in Andalucía*). The energetic can take the steep 15-minute walk up to the bars and restaurants in the village secure in the knowledge that it's downhill all the way home.

To see & do nearby: Walking in the Gaucín area, visits to Ronda and the white villages, day trips to Tangier.

HOTEL RURAL BANU RABBAH

Calle Sierra Bermeja s/n, 29490 Benarrabá

Tel: 952 150 288 or 952 150 144 Fax: 952 150 005
Email: hotel@hbenarraba.es
www.hbenarraba.es

Management:	Mercedes Méndez
Closed:	January 7 – Februay 7
Bedrooms:	12 Twins
Prices:	Twin with garden view €54-60, Twin with valley view €60-66 + 7% VAT
Meals:	Breakfast €5, Lunch/Dinner €13 excluding wine

Directions: From Estepona AP7 (peaje/toll road) towards Algeciras. Take first exit, after just 5 kms, for Casares/Gaucín. Arrving in Gaucín turn right towards Ronda on the A369. After 4.5 kms turn right down hill to Benarrabá. Hotel is at far end of village: signposted.

Málaga Province · Map 5 · HOTEL 054

Although Benarrabá is just a couple of miles from Gaucín few foreigners visit the village and there are still just a handful of expat residents. Yet this is your archetypal white village and has gorgeous vistas out across the chestnut and oak forests of the Genal valley. At the far side of the village, alone on a spur, Hotel Banu Rabbah has established a reputation amongst the walking community and groups of painters as a friendly, comfortable and very reasonably priced place to stay. The building would win no prizes for its architecture but an exuberant wisteria helps soften its angular lines and half of the bedrooms, as well as the lounge/reception area, look out across the valley. They are decorated with hand-painted wooden beds, tables and dressers and have large, arched terraces. The hotel's Kábilas restaurant is just 25 yards from the main building, next to the swimming pool. The simple, country-style cooking looks to the local recipe books for inspiration and there are some interesting vegetarian dishes, too. The staff are young and friendly and the walking here is fantastic: there are waymarked routes leading straight out from the hotel or pick up a copy of my book *Walking in Andalucía*: the Walk of the Vizir's Garden begins at the hotel.

To see & do nearby: Walking in the Genal Valley, visits to the Pileta Cave, Gaucín and Ronda and other pueblos blancos (white villages).

MOLINO DEL SANTO

Barriada de la Estación s/n, 29370 Benaoján

Tel: 952 167 151/216 Fax: 952 167 327

Email: info@molinodelsanto.com

www.molinodelsanto.com

Management:	Pauline Elkin & Andy Chapell
Closed:	Early November – mid February
Bedrooms:	7 Doubles, 7 Twins and 4 Suites
Prices:	Double €90-140, Superior Double €95-160, Suite €100-180 including VAT. Half board obligatory during High Season.
Meals:	Breakfast included, Lunch/Dinner €35 per person per night

Directions: From Ronda A374 towards Sevilla for approximately 2 kms then left on MA-5055 towards Benaoján. After 10 kms cross railway and river bridges then turn left for Estación de Benaoján and follow signs to Molino.

Pauline Elkin and Andy Chapell have gradually built Molino del Santo up to its model small hotel status thanks to more than a dozen years of hard work and good will. The physical setting is magnificent: right beside the rushing mountain torrent that once powered the mill's waterwheels, surrounded by exuberant vegetation and with views out to the rocky hillsides of the Guadiaro valley. Guests return time and time again because of the friendliness of the staff and the reassurance of known-standards in Molino's restaurant – one of the first in the area to make real efforts to buy organic local produce – and in its bedrooms which are redecorated and improved at the end of every season. Andy and Pauline's hotel is the proof that ethics and business can be happy bedfellows. Come here to walk, to visit Ronda and the white villages or just to relax beneath the willows to the sound of the rushing water which once powered the millstones. Andy is also a keen ornithologist and has sponsored a field guide to the birds of the area. But book your room as soon as possible: the word is already out about this magical world of shady corners, crystalline spring waters and solid comfort.

To see & do nearby: The Pileta Cave, walking and guided ornithological tours in the Grazalema Natural Park, visits to Ronda and the white villages.

POSADA DEL FRESNO

Calle Miguel de Cervantes 2, 29360 Montejaque

Tel: 952 167 544 or 649 972 979 Fax: 952 167 327

Email: posadadelfresno@terra.es

www.posadadelfresno.com

Management:	Romi Suárez Parellada & Ángel Martínez García
Closed:	Never
Bedrooms:	1 Double and 3 Twins
Prices:	Double/Twin €60 including VAT
Meals:	Breakfast included, Picnic lunch €8, Lunch/Dinner €15 including wine.

Directions: From Ronda A374 towards Sevilla for approximately 2 kms then left on MA5055 towards Benaoján. Here continue straight across roundabout then on to Montejaque. Follow road straight into village to the main square and church. From here call Ángel on mobile who will come to square, guide you to Posada, then help you to park.

It makes a refreshing change to come across Spanish rather than foreign incomers in an Andalusian mountain village. Angel, an amiable *sevillano*, and Romi, an effusive *catalana*, fell for Montejaque and its spectacular surroundings several years ago and decided to make a break from city life. They first ran a bar on the sleepy main square before converting an old house, tucked away in a quiet corner of the village, to create an inn concieved in true *posada* tradition: a simple lodging where travellers will find a comfortable bed, wholesome food and affordable prices. The decoration is authentically *andaluz* with beamed and planked ceilings, waferbrick floors, and photos and prints of the surrounding mountains. Furnishings, too, are in synch with *Times Past*: wooden tables, chairs and cabinets made by local carpenters and wrought iron bedsteads. Neither the dining room nor the bedrooms are big on space but the atmosphere is snug and welcoming, especially in winter when the central heating kicks in. There is a high-ceilinged sitting room with a collection of books on the Park, some of them written by Angel who is a passionate caver and walker: heed his advice on the best hikes out from Montejaque. Given warning Romy could have a *paella* waiting for you on your return and may recite one of her poems, inspired by her adopted *pueblo blanco*.

To see & do nearby: The Cueva de la Pileta and Cueva del Gato, walking in the Grazalema Park, day trips to Ronda and the train journey south along the Guadiaro river valley.

EL TEJAR & DAR HAJRA

Calle Nacimiento, 29430 Montecorto

Tel: 616 057 184 Fax: 952 167 327

Email: info@rondatejar.com

www.rondatejar.com or **www.darhajra.com**

Management:	Guy Hunter-Watts
Closed:	Never
Bedrooms:	2 Houses with own pools: El Tejar sleeping 6-8, Dar Hajra sleeping 2-4. Weekly lets from Saturday to Saturday.
Prices:	Larger house: €1500-1750, Smaller House: €1150-1350 including daily help. Reductions for longer bookings.
Meals:	Self-catering and housekeeper can prepare meals.

Directions: From Ronda A374 towards Sevilla. Exit for Montecorto then take cobbled track opp. church for 'Bar La Piscina'. At end of track turn right. Head up hill, pass left of house no. 54 then at last house go sharp right up track through pines. Track soon descends to E.T./D.H..

If you prefer self-catering to being catered for then El Tejar or Dar Hajra could provide you with a very special base, especially if walking is your thing. These are the two highest houses in the pretty, whitewashed village of Montecorto, just to the west of Ronda, and they have magnificent views out to the peaks of the Grazalema National Park. Both houses have been regularly featured in design magazine articles and are quite different in feel. El Tejar is a traditional converted farmhouse with beams and terracotta floors and four en suite bedrooms whilst Dar Hajra is much more contemporary in feel, a spectacular two bedroom house which wraps round a rocky outcrop, whence its name: Dar Hajra means 'House of the Rocks' in Arabic. Neither house is visible from the next and they are surrounded by a lovely swathe of mature garden where almond, olive, palm and orange trees, bamboo, jasmine and bougainvillaea provide a real visual feast. Each house has its own pool: El Tejar's is round (pictured here) and spring-fed whilst that of Dar Hajra is of just plunge dimensions with a spectacular infinity edge that leads the eye out to the Grazalema mountains. The houses have masses of books, CDs, computers with 24 hour Internet access and included daily help. See websites for more details. *Interior photo shows Dar Hajra's sitting room.*

To see & do nearby: Walking in the Grazalema Park, visits to the Roman theatre of Accinipo, the Pileta Cave, Ronda and the white villages.

CORTIJO LAS PILETAS

Ctra Antigua de Montejaque km 0,5, 29400 Ronda

Tel: 605 080 295 Fax: 952 854 018

Email: info@cortijolaspiletas

www.cortijolaspiletas.com

Management:	Elisenda Vidal & Pablo Serratosa
Closed:	November & January
Bedrooms:	5 Doubles, 3 Twins, 1 Family Room and 1 Family Room with 2 connecting bedrooms
Prices:	Double/Twin €80-90, Family Room for 3 €98-126 or Family Room with 2 connecting bedrooms €160-170 + 7% VAT
Meals:	Breakfast included, Picnics €8, Dinner €30 excluding wine, by prior arrangement.

Directions: From Ronda A374 towards Sevilla. Continue for 12kms (ignoring first turn to Benaoján/Montejaque) then turn left on MA8403 towards towards Montejaque. Las Piletas is first farm on the left, signposted.

Las Piletas is only a short drive from Ronda but is deeply bucolic. Elisenda and Pablo have breathed new life into the farm by converting the outbuildings of this traditional Andalusian *cortijo* to create ten superbly comfortable guest bedrooms. These look out across the pool to a marvellous sweep of farmland where Pablo has marked walking routes: this is a great area for birdwatching and tours with a local expert can be arranged. In the main farm building is a delightful dining room where dinner feels like a real celebration: the atmosphere is intimate, the tables beautifully dressed and the food and wine first class. There is also a large drawing room in the main farm building with masses of comfy chairs, sofas and an honesty bar, just the place to hunker down with a good novel. It is wonderful to sit in the evening and contemplate the changing light on the hillsides from the bedroom terraces, perhaps watching the *retinto* cattle returning home for the night. You are just a quarter of an hour from Ronda and the pretty white village of Montejaque is only ten minutes away. Everybody who stays as a guest of Pablo and Eli wax lyrically about their stays and many return year after year.

To see & do nearby: Birdwatching, Ronda and the white villages, walking in the Grazalema Park.

FINCA NARANJA

          @

Peña Cerrada 42, Ronda La Vieja, 29400 Ronda

Tel: 952 870 476 or 666 153 906 Fax: 951 232 394

Email: info@fincanaranja.com

www.fincanaranja.com

Management:	Conchita Kien
Closed:	Never
Bedrooms:	1 Suite and 2 luxury Suites
Prices:	Suite for 2 €110, Luxury Suite for 2 €145 + €45 per extra person including VAT
Meals:	Breakfast included, no other meals. Many excellent restaurants in Ronda.

Directions: From Ronda A374 towards Sevilla then right for Setenil/Acinipo. After 4.5 kms turn right and at fork follow orange signs to Finca Naranja.

A spectacular winding road cuts up from the Ronda valley, by way of ancient oak forests, to the Roman theatre of Acinipo. Just to the north, in a hidden valley, amidst groves of olive, almond and walnut, Conchita Kien has fashioned a supremely comfortable and stylish series of living spaces in her stone-clad *casita* suites. Cool marble floors, Indian throws, natural stucco, shining aluminium sinks and state-of-the-art taps and fittings have been perfectly orchestrated: no surprise to learn that Conchita is an architect with eastern connections. Her sense of space, light and 'what works' is manifest in every corner. Come to Finca Naranja to leave the mundane behind, to abandon yourself to the changing light on the fields that roll away from the farm up towards Acinipo, to unwind and to recharge those inner batteries. Conchita's orange dream strikes just a perfect balance between respecting your intimacy (breakfast is delivered to you to enjoy in the privacy of your *casita*) and a willingness to help you see the very best of what is local. This area is now producing some excellent wines so be sure to include a visit to a local bodega or two and, of course, find time to visit the Roman theatre.

To see & do nearby: The Roman ruins of Acinipo, cycling and walking, Ronda and the white villages.

HOTEL MOLINO DEL ARCO

Partido de los Frontones s/n, 29400 Ronda

Tel: 952 114 017 Fax: 952 114 457

Email: info@hotelmolinodelarco.com

www.hotelmolinodelarco.com

Management:	Juan Clavero Fernández de Córdova
Closed:	Never
Bedrooms:	4 Doubles, 9 Junior Suites and 2 Suites
Prices:	Double €130, Junior Suite €180, Suite €245 + 7% VAT
Meals:	Breakfast €12, Lunch/Dinner €50

Directions: From San Pedro de Alcántara A397 then A374 bypassing Ronda towards Sevilla. Shortly past the turning for Benaoján (don´t take this road!) between km posts 117 and 116 turn right. Go under bridge and then left at first fork. Cross a small bridge and after approx. 200 metres left again at sign for hotel. Signposted.

Málaga Province · Map 5 · HOTEL 060

During these past decade the mountains surrounding Ronda have seen a huge increase in the number of 'small is beautiful' hotels. And opting for rural/rustic no longer implies leaving your creature comforts behind or kipping in the hay. Just a ten minute drive from the town yet deeply bucolic Molino del Arco is amongst the very best of them. The old olive mill and its dependencies were revamped and refurbished following the brief of the local architect 'Quique' Santos Buendía. Natural renders, wafer-bricking, cool olive shades and contemporary art have been smoothly orchestrated to create an atmosphere of peaceful, solid comfort. The bedrooms, each named after a different variety of olive, have rich fabrics, painted white beams, coco matting and subtle lighting: flat screened TVs would be a plus for some of us whilst the gorgeous *tadlakt* (polished stucco) bathrooms will be appreciated by all. Beyond the main drawing room is a pretty cobbled patio which leads out to an extraordinary terraced water garden with a huge pool at its lower end. This is a magical place to be at night and the food – 'creative Andalusian cuisine' – is exceptionally good.

To see & do nearby: Ronda and the white villages, walking, Acinipo and the Pileta cave.

MOLINO DEL PUENTE

Calle Fuente de la Higuera 7, Bajo, 29400 Ronda

Tel: 952 874 164 or 667 433 887 Fax: 952 879 078

Email: info@hotelmolinodelpuente.com

www.hotelmolinodelpuente.com

Management:	Elaine & Ian Love
Closed:	December 10-20, January 10-31
Bedrooms:	2 Twins, 3 Doubles, 1 Family Room and 4 Superior Doubles
Prices:	Double/Twin €70-95, Family Room €110-135, Superior Double €110-135 + 7% VAT
Meals:	Breakfast included, Lunch/Dinner €20

Directions: From Ronda take A374 towards Sevilla. After approximately 7kms, just past the Don Benito Hotel, turn right at Km 26. Follow this road past Don Benito hotel then at a fork bear left. The hotel car park is immediately to your right.

Elaine and Ian's names may ring a bell in the ears of some readers of this book: they owned and managed the Harbour Lights restaurant in Puerto Cabopino. After waving goodbye to the *Costa* and a devoted clientele they headed for the Ronda hills where they converted a three hundred year old mill house to create a 10 bedroom hotel, in the lee of the bridge from which it takes its name. A convivial bar doubles as reception where you'll be greeted with Elaine's lovely smile: its time to relax and slip into that 'let's have a good time' mood. The hotel wraps around two courtyards, one in traditional *cortijo* style with a central fountain, the other looking out across the dining terrace to the pool and the Guadalcobacín river. Vestiges of the old mill can still be seen in the dining room where a sculptural central hearth provides the visual focus and paintings by local artists hang on the walls. The food is really good, a commingling of Spanish and International cuisine and the wine list is one of the best in the *sierra*: the Loves love wine. Most of the Molino's guest bedrooms look out to the garden and pool. They are generous on space, attractively furnished in cosy-rustic style and have swish bathrooms, some of them with jacuzzi tubs. *Wine tasting courses and other theme weekends are often organised: call for details.*

To see & do nearby: Trips into Ronda, walking in the Sierra de las Nieves and the Grazalema mountains, wine tastings at local bodegas.

LA FUENTE DE LA HIGUERA

Partido de los Frontones, 29400 Ronda

Tel: 952 114 355 Fax: 952 114 356

Email: info@hotellafuente.com

www.hotellafuente.com

Management:	Christina & Pom Piek
Closed:	Never
Bedrooms:	3 Standard Doubles, 7 Suites and 1 Suite for 4
Prices:	Twin €148, Junior Suite/Artist's Suite €166, Suite €180, Deluxe Suite €196, Suite for 4 €260 + 7% VAT
Meals:	Continental breakfast included, Light Lunches €17.50, Dinner €45 excluding wine.

Directions: From San Pedro de Alcántara A397 to Ronda then A374 following signs for Sevilla. Shortly past the turning for Benaoján (don´t take this road!) turn right at km post 28 onto a narrow road. Go under bridge and after 500m go left at fork. Cross small bridge and after approx. 500 metres left at sign for hotel.

When Pom and Tina headed south from Holland to convert their tumble-down olive mill, everyone else was opting for Andaluz/rustic style. They were after something spicier, something more original. So whole floors were shipped in from the Far East, there's not a twisted beam in sight and, where others might have hung a print of the Ronda bridge, there's modern art from Amsterdam. What they've achieved is a light, airy, exceptionally soothing series of spaces that seem imbued with their own open, laid-back spirit. The travel magazine Condé Nast Traveller seemed to get a finger on the pulse when they wrote about the 'chilled-out, house-party atmosphere' and Pom and Tina really do have the knack of making you feel more like house guest than client. The hotel stands high on a hill surrounded by olive groves with views out across the pool to Ronda. At night it is simply magical here. Bedrooms (most of them suites) are huge and colonial-style furniture is nicely contrasted against their clean, unfussy lines. The set-menu dinners are excellent, the selection of wines superb and the hotel has a growing number of faithful clients. And Tina has recently opened Rise, an extraordinary hilltop luxury lodge where yoga weeks, and other courses, are regularly staged.

To see & do nearby: Riding and walking in the Grazalema and Sierra de las Nieves Natural Parks, ballooning near Ronda, visits to Ronda and the other pueblos blancos (white villages).

ARRIADH HOTEL

Camino de Laura-Ronda, Apartado de Correos 490, 29400 Ronda

Tel: 952 114 370 or 607 192 384

Email: arriadhhotel@avired.com

www.arriadhhotel.com or **www.andalucia.com/arriadh**

Management:	Ulrika Waldenström & Eduardo Tataje
Closed:	Never
Bedrooms:	5 Doubles
Prices:	Double with terrace €75, Double with balcony €65 including VAT
Meals:	Breakfast included, light Lunches approx €15, Dinner €20 excluding wine

Directions: From Ronda, at roundabout on ring-road, A357 towards Campillos. After 200 metres left towards Arriate on M428. After 4 kms, as you arrivie in Arriate take the first right, go up hill, go right again and follow track to hotel.

The valley that leads north from Ronda to Arriate is fast being populated by expats in search of the Good Life. Eduardo and Ulrika, on the run from the Swedish winters, found a spectacular location to build the small hotel of their dreams, high on a hill looking out across a verdant valley to the distant peaks of the Grazalema mountains. 'Small is beautiful' was their *principe de base* and so they built just five bedrooms where seven or eight could have fitted quite comfortably. The building's base elements are *andaluz* to the core: wafer bricks, terra-cotta tiles, locally made *appliqué* lamps and attractive wooden furniture. Beds are big, bathrooms too, and central heating throughout the building is a real plus in winter when cold winds blow down the valley. Both rooms and food are really good value compared to hotels of a similar standards. Ulrika takes time and care when preparing suppers and her set menus have a higher-than-usual salad and fish content. A friendly, comfortable small hotel which is growing in charm as the newly-planted garden gets established.

To see & do nearby: Ronda, the *pueblos blancos* (white villages) of the Grazalema Park, Ronda La Vieja and Setenil.

BARAKA

Calle Rueda Doña Elvira, 29400 Ronda

Tel: 952 872 843 or 610 390 945

Email: barakaronda@yahoo.es

www.barakaronda.com

Management:	Anahid Nazeli
Closed:	November – February
Bedrooms:	2 Twins
Prices:	Twin €75
Meals:	Breakfast included.

Directions: From San Pedro de Alcántara A397 to Ronda. Take the first entrance into the town. Pass in front of the old town walls and then bear right and upwards into the old town. Here take the last street on the right just before bridge, go down hill and try to park. At fountain bear right, house on right.

Málaga Province · Map 5 · HOTEL 064

Anahid was swept off her feet by the beauty of Ronda's old town when she came to visit some three years back. Maybe the groves of olives and oranges that grow in the valley beneath the town stirred memories of her childhood in the Lebanon. She bought a house on a whim - 'Ronda chose me' - and traded work in software training for running a cosy little B&B. The history of the house has been lost but parts of it are very old: you are, after all, at the heart of what was the old Moorish citadel and just yards from the Palacio del Rey Moro and its extraordinary *mina*, an underground passageway leading all the way down to the base of the gorge. You enter the house by way of a small patio where breakfast is served in the warmer months and where guests can help themselves from an honesty bar. Anahid's stencilled onion-domed arches suggest Eastern promise and you'll be comfortable in either of her two guest bedrooms. She has decorated them with a distinctly feminine touch: her own handpainted floral friezes, cool cotton bedspreads, antique bedsteads and gentle pastel tones. Both have small shower rooms. Although the only public space is a tiny dining room you have Ronda right on your doorstep.

To see & do nearby: La Casa del Rey Moro, the Arab baths and the Mondragón Palace.

HOTEL SAN GABRIEL

Calle Marqués de Moctezuma 19, 29400 Ronda

Tel: 952 190 392 Fax: 952 190 117

Email: info@hotelsangabriel.com

www.hotelsangabriel.com

Management:	José Manuel Arnal Pérez
Closed:	January 1-7, July 21-31, December 21-31
Bedrooms:	8 Doubles/Twins, 9 Superior Doubles/Twins, 3 Junior Suites and 1 Honeymoon Suite
Prices:	Double/Twin €62-114, Superior Double/Twin €69-124, Junior Suites €77-135, Honeymoon Suite 112-183 + 7% VAT
Meals:	Breakfast €6.50, no Lunch/Dinner available. Several good restaurants and tapas bars very close to hotel.

Directions: From San Pedro de Alcántara A397 to Ronda. Take first entrance into town, pass in front of old town wall, then bear right into old town and take second street to left. Hotel is next to Plaza del Gigante: leave luggage then park.

Málaga Province · Map 5 · HOTEL 065

The owners like to describe San Gabriel as *un pequeño gran hotel*, a great little hotel. And how right they are: a stay here is most certainly much more enrichening than the normal hotel experience. This exceptionally kind Ronda family make you feel not only an honoured guest but also like a friend of the family. I remember meeting guests who emerged from their room on Christmas day to find presents beneath the tree for them! The hotel is at the very heart of the old town of Ronda, just yards from its awesome gorge and bridge. This is every inch the grand, seigneurial town house: coat-of-arms above an entrance of dressed stone, wonderful old wrought iron grilles festooned with a rampant honeysuckle and a grand sweep of staircase (rescued from the old town hall) leading up to the bedrooms. There's the an elegant, deeply comfortable drawing room with masses of books, magazines, rugs, tapestries and family photos. Just beyond is a billiards room and a tiny cinema room (with proper old cine seats) where you can watch one of your favourite oldies on DVD. The bedrooms are simply perfect and there's a cellar bar for a pre-dinner glass of wine, quite possibly in the company of the owners. This is one of my favourite hotels in southern Spain and should you stay I'll bet that it will become one of yours, too.

To see & do nearby: The Mondragón Palace, el Puente Nuevo, la Casa del Gigante, and the Santa María Cathedral.

SMALL HOTELS & INNS OF ANDALUCÍA 171

ALAVERA DE LOS BAÑOS

Calle San Miguel s/n, 29400 Ronda

Tel: 952 879 143 Fax: 952 879 143

Email: alavera@telefonica.net

www.alaveradelosbanos.com

Management:	Inmaculada Villanueva Ayala & Christian Reichardt
Closed:	December & January
Bedrooms:	1 Single, 6 Doubles and 2 Twins
Prices:	Single €65, Double/Twin without terrace €85-95, Double/Twin with terrace €95-105 including VAT
Meals:	Breakfast included, light Lunches €14, Dinner €25-30 incl. wine. Restaurant closed Sat-Tues.

Directions: From San Pedro A397 to Ronda. Here, opposite the Parador, go right into Calle Rosario. Right at the end descend to Fuente de los Ocho Caños. Here go left, then first right, before crossing bridge to Arab Baths and hotel.

Málaga Province · Map 5 · HOTEL 066

Alavera de los Baños literally means by the side of the Arab Baths' and this small hotel stands cheek-by-jowl with what is probably Andalucía's best preserved *hammam*. When Christian and Inma, the hotel's young owners, first set eyes on the place, there was just a crumbling ruin here, but thanks to masses of hard work and the *savoir faire* of a local architect, Alavera has become a favourite stopover. The decorative style of the dining room and the bedrooms is evocative of Andalucía's Moorish past. Kilims, lamps and mosaic-topped tables were shipped in from the Maghreb and the colour washes are reminiscent of the earthy colours of that part of the world. The restaurant, whose culinary slant is also towards the flavours of north Africa, is superb although it now only opens just three days a week. Bedrooms are small but space has been imaginatively used: showers rather than baths and small sinks with handmade ceramic tiles were an attractive and practical space-saving solution. But what you most remember after a stay here is the easy, relaxed manner of Christian and Inma who make a stay here doubly special. And their garden, which looks out to fields and mountains, is a heavenly spot at any hour of the day and a good base from which to explore Ronda which is just a ten minute drive from the hotel.

To see & do nearby: The Arab baths, the Plaza de Toros, La Casa del Rey Moro and La Mina.

LA CASA GRANDE DE ALPANDEIRE

Calle Barranco 76, 29460 Alpandeire

Tel: 952 180 400 or 629 564 784 Fax: 952 180 400

Email: info@hotelcasagrande.es

www.hotelcasagrande.es

Management:	Jesús Galindo Sánchez & Rosa Barrera Bel
Closed:	Never
Bedrooms:	2 Twins and 8 Doubles
Prices:	Double/Twin €50 including VAT
Meals:	Breakfast included, Lunch/Dinner approx. €25

Directions: From Ronda towards Algeciras on A369. After 7kms turn left for Alpandeire. The hotel is behind the church, signposted.

Málaga Province · Map 5 · HOTEL 067

Its amazing how many small hotels have sprung into life in the Andalusian *sierras* thanks to that pot of gold at the end of the EEC rainbow. La Casa Grande is amongst the best, a beautifully restored 18th century village house in one of the prettiest of the Alto Genal villages. The soul of the the hotel is the natural warmth of its young custodians Rosa and Jesús who make your stay here doubly special. La Casa Grande's most memorable feature is its cosy bar and vaulted restaurant which is making big waves amongst the local and expat community. Jesús has elaborated a fabulous menu which includes a big choice of interesting salads, traditional dishes from the Genal like roasts and *revueltos*, as well as his own more innovative recipes: try his 'confit of duck with a cherry sauce' and you'll be an instant convert. The same 'keep-it-local' philosophy is the touchstone for the wine list which includes Ronda's prize-winning wines and other good regional bottles. The only downside on the food front is that you need to book ahead at weekends to stand a chance of getting a table. And La Casa Grande's bedrooms are no afterthought; prettily decorated in rustic style with sparkling shower rooms they give onto the *patio andaluz* or look out across the Genal valley. They are all that you need and more, and come with a very modest price tag.

To see & do nearby: Day trips to Ronda, Gaucín and the coast, walking in the Genal valley, swimming in natural rock pools along the the Genal river.

LA CASA DEL LLANETE

Calle Doctor Duarte 10, 29460 Alpandeire

Tel: 951 166 057 or 636 552 003 Fax: 951 166 057

Email: info@casadellanete.com

www.casadellanete.com

Management:	Nicky Duirs & Phil Burgess
Closed:	Never
Bedrooms:	3 Twin/Doubles and 1 Apartment
Prices:	Double/Twin sharing bathroom €56, Double/Twin with own shower room €60, Apartment €65 including VAT
Meals:	Breakfast included.

Directions: From Ronda towards Algeciras on A369. After 8kms turn left for Alpandeire/Ruta del Legado de Fray Leopoldo. Arriving in Alpandeire park behind church, go down steps, pass phone box, road widens to become cobbled: house no.10 is on right.

Málaga Province · Map 5 · HOTEL 068

The villages of the Alto Genal valley have recently begun to attract their first foreign *vortrekkers*. It's a mystery why they were so long in coming: this string of high *pueblos blancos* are close to Ronda, have soaring views south and are wrapped round by a swathe of glorious wooded countryside cut through by crystalline brooks and rivers. Nicky and Phil happened upon an old house at the western end of the valley once owned by the village doctor and built on the one piece of flat land in the village – whence 'Llanete'. They have fashioned a small B&B offering guests simple no-frills comfort, a home-from-home and a warm welcome. A number of original features remain – tiles, beams and doors – and Nicky has added a more contemporary splash with several of her paintings which hang alongside richly-coloured kilims. If you're feeling creative she can provide painting and drawing materials, as well as tuition, in the attic studio. And Llanete could be a good base for walking: Phil has detailed route notes for several itineraries in the valley and can even give you a massage on your return home where a small sitting room with books and DVDs, a wood burner and Maya, the Genal's most adorable hound, awaits you. A studio for self-catering lets was being added as we went to press. *Workshops and retreats ocasionally held. Details on request.*

To see & do nearby: Day trips to Ronda, the Pileta cave, walking in the Genal Valley and the Grazalema Park, exploring the villages of the Alto Genal.

HOTEL BANDOLERO

Avenida Havaral, 29462 Júzcar

Tel: 952 183 660 or 640 092 242 Fax: 952 183 660
Email: reservations@hotelbandolero.com
www.hotelbandolero.com

Management:	Ivan Sastre Pascual & David Nuyen
Closed:	2 weeks in February
Bedrooms:	2 Doubles, 4 Superior Doubles and 2 Suites
Prices:	Double €63, Superior Double €73, Suite €90 + 7% VAT
Meals:	Breakfast included, Lunch/Dinner approx. €25. Restaurant closed on Mondays.

Directions: From Ronda A397 towards to San Pedro. After 11kms, just before petrol station, turn right for Cartajima/Júzcar/Parauta. Follow road past Cartajima. Hotel is on right as you arrive in the village.

Málaga Province · Map 5 · HOTEL 069

You're forgiven if you've never heard of Júzcar, a tiny village reached by way of a serpentine road that winds round the upper reaches of the Genal valley. This was once *bandolero* country: vast tracts of tortuous limestone terrain stretch away to the north and to the south thick stands of chestnut forest, a perfect redoubt for desperate men. The architecture and decoration of this small inn follow the dictates of the local vernacular: terracotta tiles, wooden beams, rustic style furniture and a plethora of agricultural implementalia. Bedrooms are decorated in a similar 'country' vein yet come with a full quotient of creature comforts including good bathrooms, TVs, kettles and central heating: you'll appreciate it should you come to the Alto Genal in winter. But the main reason for making the detour to El Bandolero is to eat in its restaurant. Iván trained as a *cordon bleu* chef in London, worked in Conran's *Almeida* restaurant, and brings a dash of innovation to the traditional dishes of the *sierra*. How do you fancy supreme of suckling pig with a spicey honeyed sauce or tenderloin of pork stuffed with chestnuts and prunes? David will be front of house and offers good counsel when you choose your wine. He hosts occasional wine tasting weekends as well as other short breaks. *More details on request.*

To see & do nearby: The Pileta cave, Ronda, the Sierra de las Nieves, Alcornocales and Grazalema National Parks.

HOTEL LOS CASTAÑOS

Calle Iglesia 40, 29452 Cartajima

Tel: 952 180 778 or 696 081 354

Email: reservations@loscastanos.com

www.loscastanos.com

Management:	Dai Beach & John Walker
Closed:	Never
Bedrooms:	1 Single, 2 Twins and 3 Doubles
Prices:	Single €60, Double/Twin €120 + 7% VAT
Meals:	Breakfast included, snacks available at midday, Dinner (set menu) €30 including wine and coffee or €20 for a selection of tapas. No food available on Sundays.

Directions: From Ronda follow the ringroad around outskirts of town then at roundabout take the San Pedro road. After 11kms, just before petrol station, turn right at sign for Cartajima. Here enter village, bear right at rubbish bins, then take first right and park close to phone box.

When Dai Beach, having sailed the world's oceans, came looking for a Shangri-La on *terra firma* the Alto Genal was virtually unknown to foreigners. Yet this stunning wooded valley, with a handful of small villages strung out around its upper reaches, is one of Andalucía's most precious treasures, a place where you still get glances of that fabled 'real Spain'. Dai conceived the conversion of the three ancient houses that make up the fabric of Los Castaños so as to guarantee guests a maximum of space and privacy. Where she could have slotted in 8 bedrooms she opted for just six and created an enormous lounge/diner where the atmosphere is one of home-from-home: a rocking chair pulled up by the hearth, stacks of original paintings and posters, bright rugs and cushions, candlesticks and ceramics and an extensive library. This same feeling of warmth and intimacy spills over into the six guest bedrooms which strike an appealing balance between rustic good looks and solid creature comfort. You have all the makings of a perfect night away: gulp in the view over an aperitif on the roof terrace, linger over a dinner inspired in the flavours of 'western Mediterranean fusion' then sleep in deep comfort and in the silence of a village that numbers just 100 souls. When you come to leave you'll understand why Los Castaños scores so highly in those www guest-feedback rankings.

To see & do nearby: Ronda, walking in the Genal valley and Sierra de la Nieves, the Pileta cave, day trips to the coast.

AMANHAVIS HOTEL

Calle del Pilar 3, 29679 Benahavis

Tel: 952 856 026 Fax: 952 856 151
Email: info@amanhavis.com
www.amanhavis.com

Management:	Leslie & Burkhard Weber
Closed:	January 8 – February 12
Bedrooms:	3 Doubles, 3 Twins and 3 Deluxe rooms
Prices:	Standard Double/Twin €99-119, Superior Double/Twin €119-139, Deluxe rooms €149-159 + 7% VAT
Meals:	Breakfast €11, Dinner €39.90 excluding wine. Restaurant closed Sundays.

Directions: From San Pedro take the N340 towards Algeciras and then turn right for Benahavis. Follow road all the way through village; after road turns sharp right continue 25 metres and turn left and Amanhavis is on your left.

Anyone living in the Marbella area will have heard of Benahavis. This attractive medieval village, reached by way of a spectacular gorge that cuts in from the coastal road, has long been a popular gastronomic destination amongst locals, expats and holidaymakers who come to eat at one of the several restaurants that line its narrow streets. The owners of Amanhavis wanted to create something with a rather different feel and thanks to their savoir-faire and imagination their small hotel now numbers amongst Andalucía's most original places to stay. The bedrooms are an extraordinary flight of fantasy, each one of them with a different historical theme inspired by Spain's medieval period and with decoration to match. In the Astronomer's Observatory you can look up to the stars from your pillow, Sultan Boabdil's chamber feels plucked from *Arabian Nights* whilst the Catholic Kings' chamber has a more regal air. The rooms wrap round a romantic inner courtyard and plunge pool where you feast on inspired, Mediterranean cuisine accompanied by a selection of both Spanish and international wines. *The restaurant recently was included in The Telegraph's Andalusian Top Ten.*

To see & do nearby: Golf courses and a driving range, beaches, Benahavis, Puerto Banús and Marbella.

HOTEL CERRO DE HÍJAR

Cerro de Híjar s/n, Parque Natural de la Sierra de las Nieves, 29109 Tolox

Tel: 952 112 111 or 605 885 480 Fax: 952 119 745

Email: cerro@cerrodehijar.com

www.cerrodehijar.com

Management:	Guillermo González, Eugenio Llanos & Martín Jerez
Closed:	Never
Bedrooms:	7 Doubles, 7 Twins, 2 Junior Suites and 2 Suites
Prices:	Double/Twin €71-85, Junior Suite €85-99, Suite €99-109 + 7 % VAT
Meals:	Breakfast €9, Lunch/Dinner €42 excluding wine.

Directions: From Marbella A355 towards Coín. Take first turn for Monda, go through village then take MA413 for Guaro. Pass Guaro and at next junction go left on A366 towards Ronda and then left to Tolox. Follow signs for 'balneario' and here sharp right and follow signs for 2.5kms up to hotel.

What a position! If a 'room with a view' is your idea of hotel Heaven then book a night or two at Cerro de Híjar. The hotel's perch, high above the spa village of Tolox, is simply breathtaking: from here you can see for miles and miles out across the foothills and rumpled mountains of the Sierra de las Nieves. The hotel is managed by three friendly young Spaniards. One of them worked at one of the few Michelin-starred restaurants in southern Spain before bringing his culinary nous to Híjar. The food – *cocina gastronómica imaginativa* – and its presentation are simply fantastic and the prices amazing for food of this standard: you'd pay at least twice as much in London. And the bedrooms are tastefully put together, too. They have bright colour washes, Mexican furniture, Turkish wall-hangings, loads of modern art and most of them grab a glimpse of that wraparound panorama. Sierra de Híjar is a superlatively tranquil yet bright and cheery place to stay where you must, but must, be sure to have dinner. The night skies, with so little light pollution, are truly amazing and there are good walks leading straight out from here into one of the most beautiful corners of the Sierra de las Nieves Natural Park.

To see & do nearby: Walking in the Sierra de Nieves Natural Park, golf in Alahaurín, Ronda and the white villages.

HOTEL CLAUDE

Calle San Francisco 5, 29601 Marbella

Tel: 952 900 840 Fax: 952 766 272
Email: info@hotelclaudemarbella.com
www.hotelclaudemarbella.com

Management:	Désirée & Franz Wilmes
Closed:	Never
Bedrooms:	7 Doubles and 1 Suite.
Prices:	Double/Twin €230-260, Suite €340 including VAT. Room price also includes free entry to 02 Wellness.
Meals:	Breakfast included, Snacks available at any other time of the day.

Directions: Exit from A7 coastal motorway for 'Marbella Centro/Calle Trapiche'. Head south into town centre towards the sea then park in Aparcamiento El Mercado, next to the Mercado Municipal. From here take taxi or walk 5 minutes to the hotel.

Málaga Province · Map 5 & 6 · HOTEL 073

Marbella's old town is one of loveliest on the Mediterranean coast, a plexus of quiet, narrow alleyways and tiny squares: it feels light years away from the sprawling peripheral growth. Hotel Claude has only recently seen the light of day, the fruit of an inspired and meticulous restoration project overseen by Franz and Désirée Willmes. They named their hotel after the opera singer Claude Devoize who once lived here, a time when it thronged with aspiring *literati* and musicians. This is 'boutique hotel' at its best: seven gorgeous bedrooms, each with a style of its own, embracing a columned patio where a single quilted purple pouffe provides a funky visual focus. Sheets are of fine Egyptian cotton, floors are marbled, parquet or tiled, furnishings mostly angular, chic and Catalan and, like the choice of fabric, take their cue from the name of the room: Francesca, Savannah, Oriental and so on. Most bathrooms are open-plan, some with claw footed tubs, and all have stylish sinks and a range of Molton Brown goodies. For technophiles there's an iPod doc, flatscreen TV and wifi. Leading off from the patio is a manicured drawing room-cum-library and ritzy dining room where 7 square tables, one for each room, are lined up diner-style and where in-house chef Tell performs his culinary alchemy. Ask if you'd like dinner, or breakfast, sent up to Claude's roof terrace. *Room price includes free use of 02 gym and pool.*

To see & do nearby: Golf courses and watersports, visits to Benahavis, Málaga and Puerto Banus, wandering the quiet streets of the old town of Marbella.

THE TOWN HOUSE

Calle Alderete 7, Plaza Tetuán, 29600 Marbella

Tel: 952 901 791 Fax: 952 901 791

Email: info@townhouse.nu

www.townhouse.nu

Management:	Irene Westerberg
Closed:	Never
Bedrooms:	6 Doubles and 3 Twins
Prices:	Double/Twin €110-130 including VAT
Meals:	Breakfast included, no other meals. Some of the best restaurants on the coast within walking distance.

Directions: From Málaga AP7/A7 towards Cádiz then exit at km 184 for Marbella Centro Urbano. Continue along Avenida Severo Ochoa then turn right at sign for Hotel Lima. Park at first underground car park marked with 'P' then walk to hotel asking for 'Plaza Tetuán'.

Málaga Province · Map 5 & 6 · HOTEL 074

Kjell Sporong has already brought his designer's creativity to bear on the Beach House (also in this guide) which saw a complete and stunning metamorphosis some years back. At his Town House, at the heart of Marbella's attractive old town, he has again fashioned an ambience of cool elegance with a big dash of designer *chic*. Stepping in from a lively, pedestrianised street marble floors offer cool respite from the summer heat. Just beyond reception is a bar and lounge with leather sofas, interesting prints of old post cards and a number of carefully placed *objets*: ostrich eggs, glass bottles, a few potted palms, all of them positioned for maximum aesthetic appeal. The bedrooms are on three floors and are as elegant as the rest of the hotel. Fabulous beds with Scandinavian mattresses and duvets, silk curtains, marble floors, perhaps a leather armchair. My first choice would be no 9 which is tucked up under the eaves with its own private terrace. A stay at the Town House might well win you over to Marbella which, in spite of all the peripheral development, still retains oodles of charm in this part of town. And when it comes to eating out, you can choose amongst several of Andalucía's best restaurants including *Zozoï* which is just yards from The Town House.

To see & do nearby: Puerto Banus and Marbella, beaches and watersports, day excursions to Ronda.

LA POSADA DEL ANGEL

Calle Mesones 21, 29610 Ojén

Tel: 952 881 808 Fax: 952 881 810
Email: info@laposadadelangel.com
www.laposadadelangel.com

Management:	Frank Thomas
Closed:	January 10-20
Bedrooms:	10 Doubles and 7 Twins
Prices:	Double/Twin €59-93, Double with terrace €70-111 including VAT
Meals:	Breakfast €8

Directions: From Málaga take AP7/A7/E15 towards Cádiz then exit at signs for Marbella/Ojén. Take A355 to Ojén and here follow signs to village centre and park in square.

Málaga Province · Map 5 & 6 · HOTEL 075

Wonderful Ojén! So pretty, so Andalusian and yet so close to the battered Costa del Sol. You can only wonder why more expats haven't chosen the place to buy their dream home in the sun. Part of the reason, at least, is that the swathe of mountains surrounding the village has recently been declared a Unesco Biosphere Reserve, keeping the developers at bay. Should you visit the village stay at the Posada del Angel, plumb in the centre of this *pueblo blanco*. It's Breton owners, with masses of good taste and Gallic *savoir faire*, have fashioned a wonderful small hostelry from five tumbledown village houses. The spirit of the place was born of the owner's love of angels. She commissioned a remarkable series of paintings for the inn from Lorenzo Saval, an artist from Málaga. Like his angel paintings the Posada is a flight of fantasy, soaring high above the commonplace. Every room has a different mood but all exude masses of warmth and personality and are beautifully finished with superb beds and sparkling bathrooms. Perhaps most memorable of all is the colonnaded and balustraded patio with its carved columns from India and *mozarab* windows. Enchanting.

To see & do nearby: The the Sierra de Juanar Park, the wine and olive oil museums in the village, Mediterranean coast beaches just 10 minutes away.

HOTEL RESTAURANTE SANTA FE

Ctra de Monda km 3, 29100 Coín

Tel: 952 452 916 Fax: 952 453 843

Email: info@santafe-hotel.com

www.santafe-hotel.com

Management:	Marije Veugen & Jaap Schaafsma
Closed:	2 weeks in November, 2 weeks in February/March
Bedrooms:	2 Doubles and 1 Twin
Prices:	Double/Twin €66 including VAT
Meals:	Breakfast included, Lunch approx. €30, Dinner approx. €35 including wine. Restaurant closed on Tuesdays.

Directions: Leave Málaga Airport following the signs for Algeciras/Cádiz then take exit for Coín, A404. Continue following signs for Coín. Go through the villages of Alhaurín de la Torre and Alhaurín el Grande then exit for Monda/Marbella on A-355. Take the third exit A7201 towards Coín. Santa Fe is on left after 500 meters in the direction of Coín.

Málaga Province · Map 6 · HOTEL 076

Santa Fe could be just the place to stay if you are wanting both a sea and mountain holiday. You can be on the beach in just half an hour and the Sierra de las Nieves is right on your doorstep, too. The hotel is just to one side of the main road that cuts through the hills between Coín and Marbella, an old farmhouse surrounded by the groves of citrus fruit that line the Guadalhorce valley. The focus of the place in the warmer months is the poolside terrace where a huge olive tree provides welcome shade, whilst when temperatures drop a warmly decorated, beamed dining room is a wonderfully intimate spot for your meals. Foodies will enjoy Santa Fe. Its Dutch owners, Marije and Jaap, have built a solid reputation for their cuisine's mix of classic Andalusian dishes and some more innovative 'fusion' cooking which leans towards things French for inspiration. The reputation of the food is such that loads of expats drive up from the coast to eat here. The beamed, terracotta tiled bedrooms are inviting, too, and they have recently been completely redecorated. Santa Fe could be an excellent choice for a first or last night in Spain with the airport just thirty minutes down the road.

To see & do nearby: Horse-riding, walking in the Sierra de la Nieves Park, visits to Puerto Banus, Marbella and beaches.

HACIENDA DE SAN JOSÉ

Buzón 59, Entrerrios, 29650 Mijas

Tel: 952 119 494/404 Fax: 951 313 141

Email: haciendasanjose@yahoo.co.uk

www.hotelruralhaciendasanjose.com

Management:	Nicky & José García
Closed:	Never
Bedrooms:	1 Double, 1 Twin and 5 larger Twins/Junior Suites
Prices:	Double/Twin €125, Larger Twin €150 including VAT
Meals:	Breakfast included, Dinner €20-25 excluding wine. Restaurant closed Wednesday evenings.

Directions: From Fuengirola N340 towards Marbella. Leave the N340 at Cala de Mijas exit then follow signs 'Campo de Golf'/'La Cala Golf'. Turn right at the first roundabout then after 2.9 kms turn right again towards Entrerrios. The hotel is signposted on the left after 1.8 kms.

Málaga Province · Map 6 · HOTEL 077

Nicky and José built and managed a successful tennis club before seeing a quieter future in their own small country-house hotel. As past hoteliers and travellers, too, they knew what they were aiming to create: a stylish, comfortable place to stay where guests would feel as if they were *en su casa*. They already had a great location: minutes from the beach yet still deeply rural, amidst a belt of avocado and citrus groves. An exuberant garden of oleander, cypress, olive, palm and plumbago lap right up to the front door and masses of climbers soften the lines of this imposing *cortijo* style building. Five guest rooms are set around a pebbled inner courtyard where a fountain murmurs: the feeling is almost cloister-like. And the bedrooms are huge, airy and light, each with its own terrace, enormous bathroom, fitted wardrobe and top-of-the-range linen and mattresses: you won't sleep more comfortably than at San José. Up a level is a large lounge, a cosy library and a brightly decorated dining room. You can expect a memorable meal at San José and won't want for good wine: Pepe has a well-stocked cellar and enjoys sharing his knowledge of things oenological with his guests. And vegetarians, too, are in for a special treat.

To see & do nearby: Nearby beaches, golf, visits to Mijas pueblo, Puerto Banus and Marbella.

THE BEACH HOUSE

Urb. El Chaparral, Ctra de Cádiz N340 km 203, 29649 Mijas Costa

Tel: 952 494 540 Fax: 952 494 540

Email: info@beachhouse.nu

www.beachhouse.nu

Management:	Carina and Stefan Andersson
Closed:	Almost never
Bedrooms:	10 Doubles and 1 Suite
Prices:	Double €125-140, Suite €175 including VAT
Meals:	Breakfast included, no other meals. Lots of local and international restaurants just a short drive.

Directions: From airport N340 towards Cádiz then right onto A7. At fork in motorway follow signs for Fuengirola/ Mijas: you rejoin the N340. Pass km post 202 and after approx. 600 metres exit for Calas de Mijas. Take N340 back towards Fuengirola. Immediately after footbridge exit on slip road to The Beach House.

Málaga Province · Map 6 · HOTEL 078

After a recent change of owners and complete decorative metamorphosis, The Beach House now numbers amongst Andalucía's most stylish small hotels. Kjell worked in the world of design in Stockholm and every last corner of this southern villa has been decorated with aesthetic appeal in mind. There's a hint of nineties minimalism, a definite debt to things Japanese and an overall feel of repose for body and mind in both the lounge/diner and in the bedrooms. The main protagonists here are the sea and sky, their colours changing with each passing hour. The Mediterranean laps up to within yards of the Beach House and its pool and terrace almost seem to fuse with the ocean. The best rooms are naturally those with sea views: the busy N340 runs close to the other side of the house and you hear passing traffic from these rooms. Carina and Stefan, The Beach House's managers, are really caring hosts and are clearly enjoying their new life in southern Europe. They prepare a wonderful buffet breakfast which includes a glass of chilled *cava* at the weekend. And they will, of course, direct you towards the best local restaurants, one of which you can reach by walking just a few hundred yards along the beach.

To see & do nearby: Watersports, beaches, riding, golf, visits to Mijas, Málaga and Marbella.

LAS ISLAS

Calle Canela Mimosa 12, Urb. Torreblanca del Sol, 29640 Fuengirola

Tel: 952 475 598 or 618 024 993 Fax: 952 661 508

Email: bookings@lasislas.info

www.lasislas.info

Management:	Omar Samaha
Closed:	January & February
Bedrooms:	6 Doubles and 5 Twins
Prices:	Double/Twin €89-99 including VAT
Meals:	Breakfast included, Lunch approx. €20, Dinner approx. €40 including wine. Restaurant closed on Sunday night.

Directions: From airport N340 towards Algeciras. Bypass Torremolinos, continue on through Benalmádena Costa then Carabajal to Torreblanca. Here, just as you pass a Chemist's, turn right at roundabout and follow the blue signs to the hotel.

Málaga Province · Map 6 · HOTEL 079

Who would ever guess that places like this could exist less than a mile from the sprawling development of Andalucía's battered *Costa*? Although you need to wind your way through a lot of new build to reach Las Islas once you drop down the steps to its poolside terrace, dripping in lush greenery, it feels as if you've arrived at a hidden tropical valley. Here are jacaranda trees, date palms, cypresses and banana trees, all providing an exotic backdrop to a huge pool and the surrounding dining terraces. The heart of this small hotel is its Fairuz restaurant and one of the kindest-hearted restauranteurs you could hope to meet, Omar Samaha. It took him less than a year to establish this as one of the top Lebanese restaurants on the coast and everything that comes out of his kitchen – grilled meats and fish, vegetarian dishes and Lebanese classics like *kafta*, *kebabs* and *tabbouleh* – is simply delicious. And the palm trees that overhang your table, the balmy *costa* nights and moonlight reflected in the pool, are a perfect compliment to the food. Omar has given the 12 garden-facing guest rooms a complete makeover, repainting, refitting and revamping them with richly coloured *sabra* silk bedspreads, lamps, bedheads and cushions from Morocco. All of the rooms have balconies, airconditioning and small shower rooms which were also about to be refitted as this guide went to press.

To see & do nearby: Golf, riding, watersports, visits to Mijas and Picasso museum in Málaga.

LA POSADA DEL CONDE

Calle Barriada, Conde del Guadalhorce 16 & 18, 29550 Ardales

Tel: 952 112 411 or 952 112 800 Fax: 952 112 805

Email: info@hoteldelconde.com

www.hoteldelconde.com

Management:	Miguel Angel González Rodríguez
Closed:	Never
Bedrooms:	1 Single, 24 Twins and 1 Suite
Prices:	Single €45, Twin €60, Double with hydro-massage bath €78, Suite €180 + 7% VAT
Meals:	Breakfast €5, Lunch/Dinner €20 including wine

Directions: From Málaga A357 towards Campillos. Just past Ardales turn right at signs 'Embalses Conde del Guadalhorce/El Chorro'. Follow road straight (ignoring right turn for El Chorro) for 7 kms. You'll see hotel on right at far end of reservoir after crossing the dam.

Málaga Province · Map 6 · HOTEL 080

The first time I stayed at La Posada del Conde I felt obliged to question the bill. Could it really be so... little? The hotel's bedrooms are stylishly decorated, bathrooms are large, all of the fabrics and furnishings first class, yet their price tag is paltry compared to hotels of a similar standard elsewhere in Andalucía. And all of this in a beautiful swathe of the mountain terrain: the hotel is next to the Guadalhorce reservoir where you can fish or swim and close to spectacular walking country (although the extraordinary walkway along the side of the Chorro gorge, El Camino del Rey, is now closed). The food at the Posada is good value, too, and house specialities include stuffed sirloin of pork and lamb basted in honey. Or you could take an evening stroll along the edge of the reservoir and eat at *El Kiosco*, a restaurant that looks out across the reservoir. From here it is only an hour to the airport making this an excellent place to begin or end a holiday in Spain. A small, friendly and reliable place to stay, and the underfloor heating of all of the bedrooms makes this a great choice for a break in the colder months, too.

To see & do nearby: The Chorro gorge, the Torcal Park and, in season, flamingo watching at the Laguna de Fuente Piedra.

FUEGOBLANCO

Los Aneales, Apartado de Correos 272, 29500 Álora

Tel: 952 497 439 or 697 579 303 Fax: 952 497439

Email: enquiries@fuegoblanco.com

www.fuegoblanco.com

Management:	Sarah Nixon & Kenneth Beachill
Closed:	Never
Bedrooms:	1 Single, 2 Doubles, 2 Twins and 1 Suite sleeping up to 4
Prices:	Single €45-50, Double/Twin €69-79, Suite for 2 €97-116 including VAT
Meals:	Breakfast included, light Lunch/packed Lunch €7.50, Dinner €19.50 including wine.

Directions: From Málaga A357 towards Cártama/Campillos. Exit right for Pizarra/Álora then left to Álora. Cross river, go left at junction and at roundabout left up hill to Álora. At r'bout right towards El Chorro. Just past km 2 post turn right, pass under bridge, then right to Fuegoblanco.

Málaga Province · Map 6 · HOTEL 081

Fuegoblanco is hidden away in the fertile Guadalhorce valley just to the north of Álora, close to a railway line, with views across groves of citrus to the surrounding mountains. The valley teems with bird and animal life and since arriving at the farm Sarah and Kenneth have traded pesticides for a lawn mower, a gesture of their commitment to the ecological jewel that they have recently adopted. The 'Good Life' for these friendly Brits involves no meat, but don't expect just lentils and tofu should you stay at Fuegoblanco. Instead you are treated to imaginative vegetarian cuisine which can be adapted to any dietary requirement, whether gluton-free, low cholestorol, vegan, etc. You'll have masses of space should you stay: in your bedroom, in the 60 square metre guest lounge and on the farm itself where there are eight acres of meadows and groves waiting to be explored. Rugs from Morocco and Middle Eastern countries soften the rather unforgiving floors of reconstituted marble: sliding metal windows are slightly out of sync with traditional *andaluz* style. But these are decorative details and the soul of the house is a wholesome one. Have a leisurely picnic on the banks of the river then venture out through the surrounding hills on foot, mountain bike or horseback.

To see & do nearby: The gorge of El Chorro and the Bobastro ruins, the Lobo Park wolf sanctuary, walking, cycling and riding.

CORTIJO VALVERDE

Apartado de Correos 47, 29500 Álora

Tel: 952 112 979 or 663 313 992 Fax: 952 112 979

Email: info@cortijovalverde.com

www.cortijovalverde.com

Management:	Caroline & Ali Zartash-Lloyd
Closed:	November
Bedrooms:	3 Doubles and 4 Twins
Prices:	Double/Twin €96-118 + 7% VAT
Meals:	Breakfast included, light Lunch €5-7, Dinner €25 including apéritif.

Directions: From Málaga A357 towards Campillos then right for Álora. Right at junction and after 300 metres left for Álora. Cross river and at junction by bar 'Los Caballos' turn left towards Valle de Abalajís. Pass km 36 post, cross small bridge, pass old bus shelter then take fork immediately to right. After 200 metres sharp left uphill to Valverde.

Málaga Province · Map 6 · HOTEL 082

Heading north from Álora you follow a quiet country road that meanders its way through fields of wheat and groves of olives and almonds towards the Torcal Park. It also leads to Cortijo Valverde, a small and immensely comfortable country inn which already seems to be imbued with the kind, open natures of its new owners, Caroline and Ali Zartash-Lloyd. Little remains of the original farm apart from its cobbled *era* (threshing circle) which, like the new house and rooms, catches the breezes that blow down the valley. Valverde's most remarkable feature is an enormous pool that lies between the main house and five of the guest rooms: 30 lengths of this one and you'll have earned your supper. But what really makes Valverde sing is the chance of eating supper, *al fresco* for much of the year, on the lofty terrace as the sun dips behind the Sierra de la Nieves. Caroline is extremely modest about her food but it is simply excellent and picks and mixes amongst recipes from the Lebanon, Spain, France and Italy. There are thick soups in winter, a high salad content throughout the year, and an atmosphere which makes for easy conviviality. Ali and Caroline always join guests for desert and coffee and enthusiastically help you plan your next day's activities. Must-dos include Antequera, the Torcal park and a visit to Álora where there are lively *tapas* bars and a couple of excellent restaurants.

To see & do nearby: Visits to El Chorro gorge, the towns of Antequera, Álora, and Málaga, and El Torcal Natural Park.

CASA DOMINGO

Arroyo Cansino 4, 29500 Álora

Tel: 952 119 744 or 650 134 700 Fax: 952 119 744
Email: yvesencarine@casadomingo.be
www.casaruraldomingo.be

Management:	Carine Heirman & Yves Van den Bossche
Closed:	Never
Bedrooms:	1 Single, 1 Double, 1 Suite, 1 Apartment and 2 Studios
Prices:	Single €60-75, Double €70-75, Suite €80-85, Apartment €630-770 weekly for 2 + €35 p.p. extra, Studio €495-570 weekly including VAT
Meals:	Breakfast included (although not for studio/apartment).

Directions: From Málaga A357 towards Campillos via Cártama. 16 kms after Cártama right towards Álora then follow signs for 'Álora Estación'. At T junction cross road, head uphill on good track for about 900 metres then left to Casa Domingo.

Málaga Province · Map 6 · HOTEL 083

After many years of packing and unpacking suitcases throughout the world Carin and Yves finally decided that, instead of doing the travelling themselves, they should let the travellers come to them. Their aim was to create an atmosphere where guests would feel as relaxed as they would on a lazy Sunday (*domingo* in Spanish) afternoon. So although the house takes its name from the previous owner they saw no reason to rename it! From Casa Domingo's pool terrace and gardens, very much the focus of life here, there are exhilarating views across the valley to the pretty white town of Álora and, beyond, to the rumpled chain of mountains stretching west towards Ronda. At the back of the house is a barbecue area that you are welcome to make use of at any time, a tennis court and a *boules* pitch. And with great walks leading straight out from the house and riding available right next door this is a great choice for an active family holiday. Breakfast, the only meal on offer apart from picnic lunches, is served out on the terrace and is a generous spread: fresh juice from the orange groves you see below you in the valley, fruit salad, meats and cheeses, and bread which arrives still warm from the local baker. When it comes to eating out top of the list would probably be Abilio or Candela up in the old town. Or if you prefer not to take the car stroll down to Los Caballos for a typical *venta* supper but go easy on the *tinto*: its a steep climb back up to Casa Domingo.

To see & do nearby: Álora, visits to Ardales and the karst formations of the Torcal Natural Park, Antequera and Málaga.

HOTEL FUENTE DEL SOL

Paraje Rosas Bajas s/n, La Hoya, 29260 Antequera

Tel: 951 239 8230 Fax: 951 232 090

Email: info@hotelfuentedelsol.com

www.hotelfuentedelsol.com

Management:	Luis Lozano
Closed:	January 5 – February 5
Bedrooms:	8 Standard Doubles, 3 Superior Doubles, 2 Suites and 1 Imperial Suite
Prices:	Standard Double €150, Superior Double €180, Suite €200, Imperial Suite €250 + 7% VAT. Price includes use of all spa facilities.
Meals:	Breakfast included, Lunch/Dinner €40

Directions: From Antequera follow signs for Álora. At km 17 of A343 turn left for La Hoya. Here follow signs up hill to hotel.

Málaga Province · Map 6 · HOTEL 084

'Wellness' is one of the new buzz words on the Andalusian hotel scene and if you fancy some self-indulgence on the food front, combined with a bit of tonification of body and mind, Fuente del Sol should be high on your list. The hotel is blissfully quiet, built on a high bluff beneath a limestone ridge with soaring views out towards the southern seaboard. And wrapped into the fabric of this swanky, 14 bedroom hotel are an indoor pool, gymnasium, Turkish bath, Finnish sauna and massage room as well as a second outdoor pool and tennis court: if you make use of all of these facilities you'll have earned your supper. And it will be some supper, magicked up by in-house maestro David Muñoz who has worked in some of Spain's top restaurants, amongst them the Ritz in Madrid. His presentation is 5-star-perfect and his food is as mouthwatering as it is cosmopolitan: changing with the season it draws heavily on the hotel's organic veggie garden. There's an informative wine list, too, with a detailed description of each listing. Of the suites and bedrooms, the best are the four with views to the south. All are enormous with colonial style furniture, big wardrobes, bathrooms with double sinks and jacuzzi bath tubs and all the techno trimmings. The art work didn't do it for me, nor some of slightly garish bedwall colours, but Luis Lozano and his staff more than make up for these minor shortcomings.

To see & do nearby: Walking in the Torcal, day trips to Granada and Sevilla, beaches and watersports on the Costa del Sol.

LA POSADA DEL TORCAL

Partido de Jeva, 29230 Villanueva de la Concepción

Tel: 952 031 177 Fax: 952 031 006

Email: hotel@laposadadeltorcal.com

www.laposadadeltorcal.com

Management:	Karen & Geoff Banham
Closed:	January & February
Bedrooms:	1 Smaller Double, 2 Standard Doubles, 4 Superior Doubles, 2 Junior Suites, 1 Suite and 5 Villas with pools
Prices:	Smaller Double €115, Standard Double €150, Superior Double €190, Junior Suite €210, Suite €260 + 7% VAT
Meals:	Breakfast included, Lunch approx €25 à la carte, Dinner €35 (3 courses) excluding wine.

Directions: Exit from A45 for Casabermeja. Here right for Almogía then left for Villanueva de la C.. Here up hill then left at junction. After 1.5 kms right at sign for La Joya. Hotel on left after 3 kms.

If you like to get away from it all without leaving your creature comforts behind, then the Posada del Torcal will be your type of place. What I most like about this small hotel are its heart-stopping views and the open-plan bedrooms that have raised corner tubs where you can soak away your troubles without missing a second of the amazing panorama before you. Beds are enormous, the decoration stylishly pick-and-mixes the modern with the traditional, the terracotta tiled floors are underfloor heated and hidden away in a rustic-style cabinet is satellite TV and DVD players. Downstairs is a huge guest lounge and dining room and just beyond a swimming pool (heated in winter), a jacuzzi, a gym, an astroturf tennis court as well as a sauna where you can get that calory count back under control. Torcal's food is excellent as you might expect given that the head chef, Paul Tugwell, came here from the Savoy. There are wicked deserts, lots of vegetarian dishes and a good wine list. This is a hotel where the accent is very much on the Big Relax but with loads of extras on offer: you could have a massage, tennis or painting lessons or be guided on a walk through the extraordinary karst formations of El Torcal. The hotel also has a number of villas, all with pools, available for rental. See website for details.

To see & do nearby: Visits to Torcal Park, the gorge and lakes close to El Chorro, the towns of Antequera and Fuente de la Piedra.

CORTIJO EL PERAL

Finca Puerto El Peral, Monterroso, 29150 Almogía

Tel: 952 430 092 Fax: 952 430 781

Email: info@puertoelperal.com

www.puertoelperal.com

Management:	Hetty Van der Pol & Alan Handforth
Closed:	January & February
Bedrooms:	6 Doubles, 2 Twins and 2 Junior Suites
Prices:	Double/Twin €140-180, Double 'Royale' €160-190 + 7% VAT
Meals:	Breakfast included, light Lunch €10-15, Dinner €35 excluding wine.

Directions: From the Málaga ring road exit for Cártama on A357. Exit from A357 at km 64 for Campanillas. Left at first junction, then very next right and after 50 metres, at roundabout, go left and follow road to Almogía. Follow this road past village for 7 kms then go left at sign for Monterroso. Farm on right after 2 kms. (see website for more details)

Málaga Province · Map 6 · HOTEL 086

Head just an hour inland from Spain's scarred southern coast and you find yourself in a different world. Almogía feels remote (in fact it's only half an hour from Málaga) while Cortijo El Peral's hidden plateau, a few miles north west of the village, feels even further removed from civilisation. At the same time this small hotel is 'civilised' in the best sense of the word. Alan and Heti have created a superbly comfortable *hacienda*-style hotel where the accents lie on superb food and complete rest for body, mind and soul. The bedrooms are wonderful: they are massive with enormous beds (super king-size), wonderful linen and towels and the views out across the farm's olive and almond groves. Begin an evening at El Peral with a drink at the bar with Alan who is an easy and amiable host whilst Hetty works her culinary magic in a state-of-the-art kitchen. Her first source of inspiration is the Mediterranean, she's big on Italian and French dishes but, if the mood takes her, you may be offered a Thai meal. Or, if you fancy something more ethnic, head down the quietest of country lanes to an excellent local *venta. A sauna and a jacuzzi are soon to be added.*

To see & do nearby: The Torcal Park, the old town of Antequera, riding and walking.

HOTEL ATARAZANAS

Calle Atarazanas 19, 29004 Málaga

Tel: 952 121 910 Fax: 952 121 911

Email: atarazanas@balboahoteles.com

www.balboahoteles.com

Management:	Virginia Gallego
Closed:	Never
Bedrooms:	3 Doubles and 36 Twins
Prices:	Double/Twin €70-90 + 7% VAT
Meals:	Breakfast €5, Lunch/Dinner approx. €25 including wine. Restaurant closed on Sundays.

Directions: Hotel Atarazanas is next to Mercado Municipal, two streets north of the Alameda Principal, just to the east of El Corte Inglés. Nearest parking is Aparcamiento Camas, signposted as you drive along the Alameda towards the Cathedral.

Málaga Province · Map 6 · HOTEL 087

It's amazing to think how many tourists fly into Málaga airport every year and just how few visit this fascinating city - and this in spite of the recent opening of its wonderful Picasso museum. Part of the reason is the town's dearth of interesting hotels. But if you want a comfortable, safe stay at the heart of its beautiful old centre then book a room at the Atarazanas. It is slightly different in flavour to some of the hotels listed in this guide, a place that aims to attract both business folk and tourists. But the position could hardly be better, directly opposite the lively and colourful municipal market and just a short stroll from *Calle Larios* and the Cathedral. Off to one side of the reception – the staff here are extremely friendly – is a small marble-floored restaurant which doubles as breakfast room and bar. Rooms are on three floors and are comfortable rather than memorable. But the mattresses and linen are good, bathrooms immaculate and the rooms are good value considering the location. You can eat here but you'll find livelier eateries a short stroll from the hotel. It would be nice to start an evening with a sherry in the *La Antigua Casa de la Guarda* – just round the corner from Atarazanas – and then dine at the wonderful old *Las Chinitas* restaurant.

To see & do nearby: The Picasso Museum, the historic centre of Málaga, beaches and watersports.

EL RIAD ANDALUZ

Calle Hinestrosa 24, 29012 Málaga

Tel: 952 213 640 or 650 656 500

Email: elriadandaluz@hotmail.com

www.elriadandaluz.com

Management:	Florence & Florent Collobert
Closed:	Never
Bedrooms:	1 Single, 1 Twin, 4 Doubles and 2 Triples
Prices:	Single €55-60, Double/Twin €55-75, Triple €72-85 including VAT
Meals:	Breakfast €3 by arrangement with café on the Plaza de la Merced

Directions: The Riad Andaluz is on the right hand side of Calle Hinestrosa, one street northwest of the Teatro Cervantes. Best to park in Alcazaba or Granados car parks then continue by taxi. The Riad also has its own parking spaces @ €10 daily. Email for further details.

Málaga Province · Map 6 · HOTEL 088

Florence and Florent, thinking 'Small is Beautiful', gave up succesful business careers in France to open a small B&B in Málaga's old centre, a few yards from the Cervantes theatre and just around the corner from the Plaza de la Merced and the house where Picasso made his debut on the world stage. The naming of this old town house, and its decoration, was inspired by their love of the Maghreb: it seems only right that a town that saw nearly eight centuries of Islamic presence should pay lip service to that legacy. And it's no coincidence that the house follows the dictates of traditional *riad* architecture, wrapping round a plant-filled inner patio with bedrooms giving onto this inner sanctum. There are just eight, medium to small in size, simply furnished and decorated with mirrors, pictures, rugs and lamps from North Africa. Small shower rooms, with screed floors are partitioned off within the rooms. The oriental theme spills over into a small *salon marrocain* leading off from the patio, just the place for a mint tea in the afternoon and for quizzing your hosts about where to eat and what to see. No meals are served but Florent and Florence have arranged for guests to be given breakfast at a lively café on the Plaza de la Merced.

To see & do nearby: The Picasso museum and Teatro Cervantes right on your doorstep, exploring the narrow streets of the old town, walks along the beach at La Malagueta.

HOTEL LOLA

Casas de Campos 17, 29001 Málaga

Tel: 952 579 300 Fax: 952 228 265

Email: lola@room-matehotels.com

www.room-matehotels.com

Management:	Lola Martín Fenech
Closed:	Never
Bedrooms:	38 Standard Twin/Doubles, 9 Executive Twin/Doubles and 3 Junior Suites
Prices:	Standard Double €80-90, Executive Double €90-100, Junior Suite from €140 + 7% VAT. Check www. for offers.
Meals:	Breakfast included

Directions: Follow signs for 'Centro Ciudad'. Pass the Corte Inglés store then cross river into La Alameda. Take the third right into Calle Tomás de Heredia, then third right into Casas de Campo. Pass hotel, take second left, then first left and left again to hotel's car park.

I've always been wary of including places belonging to larger groupings within these pages. But Room Mate's guiding philosophy breaks the mold, attempting to imbue each of their hotels with the character of a fictitious personality. So meet Lola, a 'vivacious, sensual and passionate' young woman who lives next door to the Picasso museum. All a tad pretentious, perhaps, but this hotel fills a gap in what has been a very tired hotel scene in Málaga: it is comfortable, friendly and very good value. You check in to the sounds of chill music at a low desk covered in white ribbed leather. The receptionists look more like waiters from a Conran restaurant: you'd be forgiven for asking for a Perrier instead of your room number. A glass wall and stainless steel porthole draw a visual boundary between you and the breakfast room/bar where banks of leather benches, white bucket seats and a long sweep of black marble bar could be straight out of a 70s Bond film. Bedrooms pull just as many decorative punches with an eclectic combination of glass, leather, stainless steel and funky bedwalls. As in all R.M. bedrooms there will be a single green apple on your bedside table as well as plasma TV, Internet point and a list of recommended tapas bars and restaurants. The sort of places that Lola would like...

To see & do nearby: The Picasso museum, the Cathedral, lively bars and restaurants, trips out to the beaches east of Málaga, walking in the Axarquía.

HOTEL RURAL LA PALOMA

Ctra A-33 km 633, 29315 Villanueva de Tapia

Tel: 952 750 409 Fax: 952 750 409

Email: info@hotelrurallapaloma.com

www.hotelrurallapaloma.com

Management:	Elena d'Orso & Filippo Lapini
Closed:	End of November
Bedrooms:	8 Twin/Doubles
Prices:	Double/Twin €45-60 including VAT
Meals:	Breakfast included, Lunch/Dinner approx. €25. Restaurant closed on Monday nights.

Directions: From Málaga A92-M motorway towards Granada. Take exit 1 for Salinas/Villanueva de Tapia then follow signs for Villanueva de Tapia-Iznajar. The hotel is signposted to the right after approximately 4kms.

Málaga Province · Map 6 · HOTEL 090

Travelling home from Granada to Ronda I remembered a reader's recommendation. It was for a small roadside hotel hidden away in the olive groves north of Antequera and had waxed lyrically about the food and charming young owners. I'm glad I made the diversion. Elena and Filippo have infused this small roadside inn with their natural warmth and it has already become something of an institution amongst local expats, most of them from somewhere north of the Channel. You arrive by way of a large lounge and bar which doubles as the reception where you are greeted with a smile by Elena and handed your key. All of the eight bedrooms are on the first floor and look out across the surrounding olive and almond groves. The best are numbers 7 & 8 - the furthest from the road - but at night there's little passing traffic and all rooms are spotlessly clean with pretty fabrics, pastel colours and beautifully crafted wooden doors and windows. But the heart of this small hotel is the glass-fronted restaurant which spans out from the main building and offers superbly presented gourmet cuisine for half of what it would cost down on the *Costa*. Filippo's Italian roots are reflected in his menu which is Mediterranean with a big 'M' and includes homemade pasta, a high fish content, fresh herbs and interesting salads. You could base yourself here and head off to Granada, Málaga, Antequera and Archidona, all of which are within easy reach.

To see & do nearby: Day trips to Granada, Córdoba, Sevilla and Málaga, the Torcal Park, extensive Roman remains in Antequera.

LAGAR PADRE AVILÉS

Lagar Padre Avilés, Ctra de Olias km 7.5, 29197 Málaga

Tel: 952 294 242 or 666 148 149 Fax: 952 294 242

Email: dave_claireparish@yahoo.co.uk

www.padre-aviles.com

Management:	Claire & David Parish
Closed:	Never
Bedrooms:	7 self catering Apartments sleeping 2-7
Prices:	Apartment €125-200 according to size and season. Minimum stay 2 nights. More details on request.
Meals:	None generally available although meals can occasionally be prepared for larger groups.

Directions: From airport N340/E15 towards Motril/Almería. Pass exit for El Palo (246A) then take exit 246B onto M24 towards La Cala del Moral/Olias/El Candado. After just 1 km take exit 5 and at T junction turn right towards Olias. Lagar Padre Avilés on right after 6.5 kms.

Málaga Province · Map 6 · HOTEL 091

Claire and David, after years of sailing the world's oceans, decided to return to *terra firma* in the country where Claire spent much of her childhood. It's easy to see why they should have fallen for this old bougainvillaea-clad farmhouse that sits proudly on a bluff with amazing panoramic views down to the coastal strip and to the glittering sea (those passing yachts must pull a few heart strings!). In one wing of this ancient *lagar* where olives were once milled they have created two enormous guest apartments and have recently added a further five just across the way from the original farmhouse. All of them are ideal for both couples and families. Their décor is cool and uncluttered with Casablanca fans to take the edge off the summer heat, woodburning stoves for the colder months and all you need for self catering. There is an enormous pool and, just beneath it, two tennis courts: a coach can come up and put you through your paces if you're having problems with getting that forehand right. But Padre Avilés really comes into its own at night when the silence is all enveloping and the coastal lights twinkle far below. Claire and David are easy, immensely affable hosts, always there to help whilst being mindful of your intimacy. And it is refreshing to meet a couple who, with a young family of their own, enjoy rather than simply tolerate other couples with kids.

To see & do nearby: Málaga & the Picasso museum, beaches and watersports, riding.

FOUNTAINHEAD

Partido del Río Terral, 29180 Riogordo

Tel: 696 183 309

Email: info@fountainheadinspain.com

www.fountainheadinspain.com

Management:	Helen Bartlett
Closed:	Mid November – mid February apart from Christmas Day & New Year's Eve. Normally closed every Wednesday night.
Bedrooms:	4 Suites
Prices:	Suite for 2 €225 including VAT
Meals:	Breakfast included, Lunch (tapas style delivered to suites) €18, Dinner €40

Directions: From Málaga A45 (N331) towards Granada. Take exit 148 for Casabermeja then go right towards Riogordo. After 19kms exit for Riogordo, go through village centre then take road towards Benarmargosa. After 2kms turn right on track: up hill, over brow, then down to F'head.

Málaga Province · Map 6 · HOTEL 092

Fountainhead is one of the few places to stay in southern Spain that radically breaks the standard hotel mold. This is a retreat hotel in the genuine sense: it stands in glorious isolation on a high north-facing bluff and its whole ethos is pitched at tranquility and privacy. Forget TV, turn off the mobile, leave the laptop behind: you're here to relax. There are 4 guest suites, with a new villa in the pipeline, each with its own patio and plunge pool. Their decoration was a flight of decorative fancy inspired by their names: Helen is a dress designer and her love of fabric and theatricality was given free rein in every corner. There are cushion-strewn beds and benches, funky art, lots of stripes, beads and tassels and above all, colour: red and black in the Oriental suite, pink and ivory for the Indian, teal and aquamarine in the Sultan and chequered lemon, orange and green in the larger Arizona suite. The lounge/diners of each suite have a *coin cuisine* where you'll find the ingredients for breakfast: home baked bread, croissants and Danish pastries are delivered on the day. If suites are remarkable, so too is the restaurant where Peter is culinary *maestro*. His food is inspired by the best Mediterranean cuisines, presentation is picture perfect and his wine list a joy. It includes an amazing selection of Spanish *crianzas* as well as a half a dozen flagship French wines, and, *bien sûr*, the best champagne.

To see & do nearby: Day trips to Málaga and Granada, walking in the Torcal Park, beaches and watersports on the Costa del Sol.

HOTEL PALACIO BLANCO

Calle Felix Lomas 4, 29700 Vélez-Málaga

Tel: 952 549 174 or 652 975 341

Email: nick@palacioblanco.com

www.palacioblanco.com

Management:	Lesley & Nick Vallance
Closed:	3 days at Christmas
Bedrooms:	2 Twins and 6 Doubles
Prices:	Double/Twin €75-95 + 7% VAT
Meals:	Breakfast €7

Directions: From Málaga A7 towards Motril. Exit at junction 273 then bear left towards Vélez-Málaga. Go straight across at first roundabout, then at second roundabout turn right. At the next roundabout take the third exit into Calle Alcalde. Go straight across at the next roundabout then immediately right. Bear right at fork by florists and head up hill to hotel which is on the left.

Málaga Province · Map 6 · HOTEL 093

You may recognise the names Lesley and Nick Vallance: their odyssey in transforming this 400 year old mansion house into a boutique hotel was described over several episodes on British TV. Palacio Blanco is tucked away at the top of Vélez-Málaga and its sober white façade gives little away from the outside. But beyond the heavy wooden doors is an elegant, colonnaded patio with a sweep of staircase leading up to the bedrooms and, up another level, to a rooftop spa pool and terrace: no better place for a sundowner gazing out across the old town to the hilltop castle. The dazzling white of the walls – thus *Palacio Blanco* – serves as backdrop to a series of richly-coloured paintings inspired by flamenco dance. This same juxtaposition is carried over into the bedrooms which are deeply comfortable with the best linen sheets, big beds stacked up with bright cushions and fabulous bathrooms. I loved the studied minimalism coupled with splashes of rich colour – lots of gold and crimson – and being a bit of a technophiliac, appreciated the gadgetry; wifi, flat screen TV and a dock for the iPod. Breakfast is the time to enjoy the easy company of your hosts and hear more about the creation of P.B.. Nick does an early croissant run whilst Lesley, with infectious vivacity, advises on excursions and where to eat. As of 2008 you can take a tram just yards away straight down to the beach.

To see & do nearby: Beaches and watersports, walking in the Axarquía, day trips to Málaga and Granada.

LAGABELLA

Los Olivos, Lagabella s/n, 29715 Sedella

Tel: 649 035 387

Email: lagabella@lagabella.com

www.lagabella.com

Management:	Beatrice Truyen & Johan Ghijsens
Closed:	Never
Bedrooms:	1 Twin and 2 Doubles
Prices:	Double/Twin €66, Larger 'Manzil' Double €91 including VAT
Meals:	Breakfast included, Dinner €15-20 excluding wine, by prior arrangement.

Directions: From the A7/E15 exit for Vélez Málaga. Continue towards Viñuelas for approx. 10kms then right for Canillas de Aceituno. Here continue towards Sedella. Lagabella signposted to right after approx. 6 kms.

Málaga Province · Map 8 · HOTEL 094

Beatrice and Johan ran a restaurant in southern France before heading for the warmer climes of southern Spain. They travelled many a mile in search of their *Shangri-La* before happening upon the lowest of a small cluster of houses at the foot of the mighty Maroma mountain: from here there are sweeping views southwards towards the Med. Johan has created a series of terraces, all now awash with greenery, and a pretty, winding path that cuts up to a pool: it is shared with a couple of the houses close by although most of the time you'll have it to yourself. There are a number of shaded areas with loungers in amongst the flowers and aromatic plants, perfect places for a lazy siesta. The decoration of bedrooms was the creation of Beatrice and their bright colour coordination seem to reflect her own smiling personality. Each has its own terrace, the upper one catching those views to the south and they all shine as brightly as the newest pin. But the house's best feature is the lower terrace where meals are served. As you might expect given the owners' culinary past, food at Lagabella is a real celebration. Breakfast is a three course banquet - Beatrice has no fewer than 18 different menus lined up - and you'll be treated to a truly memorable dinner. And both rooms and food are excellent value.

To see & do nearby: Walking in the Axarquía, the Múdejar architectural route, Alhama de Granada.

FINCA EL CERRILLO

29755 Canillas de Albaida

Tel: 952 030 444 Fax: 952 030 444

Email: info@hotelfinca.com

www.hotelfinca.com

Management:	Sue & Gordon Kind
Closed:	December apart from Christmas
Bedrooms:	11 Twin/Doubles and 1 Apartment sleeping up to 4
Prices:	Double/Twin €100-110, Apartment €100-110 + 7% VAT
Meals:	Breakfast included, Light lunches €10, Dinner (Sat, Mon, Wed and Fri) €25 excluding wine.

Directions: From Málaga A7/E15 towards Motril. Pass exit 272 for Vélez-Málaga then take next exit 277 for Algarrobo/Caleta. Head inland past Sayalonga then left to Archez. Here left towards Sedella/Salares. Cross bridge, go up hill then turn right at sign 'Fogarate'. El Cerrillo is on right before you reach Canillas. If in doubt on this final section keep right.

Canillas de Albaida is one of the prettiest villages of La Axarquía. Narrow streets wind up to its lovely hilltop chapel and the lush, subtropical valley that cuts north from here into the Sierra Tejeda is an absolute 'must-walk'. The hillsides around the village are peppered with small-holdings and one of the loveliest of them, the ancient olive mill of El Cerrillo, has recently been converted into a wonderful small inn by its young English owners. The position is stunning: there are massive views down towards the sea and a wonderful mature garden whose botanical highlights are the palms and an ancient carob. El Cerrillo has already made its name amongst the walking community but this is great place to chill out, too. There are stacks of books in the library (ask Gordon for the history of the remarkable armchair!) a massive beamed lounge-cum-dining room and hidden corners in the garden where you can lounge your day away gazing out across the valley. The food is excellent - if you're feeling sociable it can be served at one large table - and the bedrooms are simply fabulous with the swishest of bathrooms. A number of groups now use the place as a base: they come to write, walk and paint in this uniquely beautiful setting. More details from Sue and Gordon.

To see & do nearby: Walking in the Sierra Tejeda and Almijarra, Competa and Nerja.

LA POSADA MORISCA

Loma de la Cruz s/n, Ctra de Montaña Frigiliana-Torrox, 29788 Frigiliana

Tel: 952 534 151 Fax: 952 534 339

Email: info@laposadamorisca.com

www.laposadamorisca.com

Management:	Sara Navas Sánchez
Closed:	Mid November – mid January
Bedrooms:	2 Doubles, 8 Twins and 2 doubles superior
Prices:	Double/Suite €50-90 + 7% VAT
Meals:	Breakfast €7

Directions: From Málaga A7/E15/N340 towards Motril then exit at km 292 for Frigiliana/Nerja. Take MA105 to Frigiliana and here go round bottom of village following signs for Torrox. 1.5 kms from Frigiliana turn left at sign for hotel: down steep track then bear left to Posada.

La Posada Morisca is just a few kilometres from Frigiliana, terraced in amongst groves of avocado and mango in one of the most fertile parts of Andalucía's coastal fringe. Although this small hotel is less than ten years old it feels as if it has been here for much longer, wrapped round by an exotic garden of palm, bougainvillaea, jasmine and rambling bignonias. The creation of this small hotel was a real labour of love for Sara and husband José Luis: Posada's bedrooms are amongst the nicest in the Axarquía, an appealing mix of the rustic - terracotta tiles, latticed wardrobes, wood-burning stoves and handmade tiles from Vélez - with the stylish: warm colours and snazzy fabrics. No two are the same and all have panoramic views out to the Mediterranean. The decoration of the restaurant in the same warm and rustic vein: wafer brick, more terracotta and a bright, ceramic-tiled bar contrasted by floral curtains and creamy-coloured walls. This would be a great place for walkers to stay: waymarked circuits pass close to the house and, beginning in Frigiliana, the amazing Liman trail cuts through a spectacular swathe of mountains all the way down to the coast. For details see my book *Walking in Andalucía*.

To see & do nearby: The caves at Nerja, the villages of Frigiliana and Cómpeta, beaches and *caletas* (coves) close to Maro.

HOTEL PARAÍSO DEL MAR

Calle Prolongación de Carabeo 22, Apartado de Correos 14, 29780 Nerja

Tel: 952 521 621 Fax: 952 522 309
Email: info@hispanica-colint.es
www.hotelparaisodelmar.com

Management:	Enrique Caro Bernal
Closed:	Mid November – mid December
Bedrooms:	10 Twin/Doubles, 3 Junior Suites and 4 Suites
Prices:	Standard Double/Twin €84-120, Double/Twin with sea view €99-135, Junior Suite €115-155, Suite with balcony and sea view €125-165 + 7% VAT
Meals:	Breakfast included, no other meals. Several local and international restaurants within an easy walk of hotel.

Directions: Round Málaga on A7/E15 then exit for Nerja. Here follow signs for the Parador: Hotel Paraíso del Mar is just a few yards away at the edge of the Balcón de Europa.

Málaga Province · Map 8 · HOTEL 097

You'll probably remember two things about Hotel El Paraiso del Mar. One will be the stunning location high above Nerja's long sweep of golden sand. The other will be meeting Enrique Caro Bernal. He is one of a rare breed of hoteliers who, even at the end of the season, is able to greet you with the same warmth and enthusiasm as he would his very first guest. Nowadays visitors will book their holidays a year in advance yet this is not a man to rest on his laurels: not a year passes without some part of his small hotel being refurbished or refurnished. Paraiso del Mar has gradually been built up round what was once the private villa of an English doctor. Later additions have been added in such a way that you'd have difficulty saying where the original building ends and the new one begins. Several bedrooms and suites have balconies and/or terraces that look out across the cliff-side, terraced gardens to the beach which can be reached by a steep path that drops down from the hotel. Without doubt this is one of the Costa's friendliest small hotels and even though Nerja is expanding fast at the edges, this part of town has retained its charm.

To see & do nearby: The Nerja caves, El Balcón de Europa, Frigiliana, walking in the Axarquía.

HOTELS 098 – 103

CÓRDOBA

CASA DE LOS NARANJOS

Calle Isabel Losa 8, 14001 Córdoba

Tel: 957 470 587 Fax: 957 470 587

Email: casadelosnaranjos@telefonica.net

www.casadelosnaranjos.com

Management:	Matilde Jiménez
Closed:	Never
Bedrooms:	20 Doubles/Twins
Prices:	Double/Twin €70-105 + 7% VAT
Meals:	Breakfast included

Directions: The hotel is very close to the 'Ayuntamiento' (Town Hall) and the Roman Temple just east of the Plaza Tendillas. Guests can use the Hotel Alfaros car park for €11 daily.

Córdoba Province · Map 7 · HOTEL 098

Finding a decent place to stay in Córdoba has never been easy, in spite of the huge number of visitors who pass through. So when I stepped in off the street and met with the smiling Matilde and was shown around this small hotel, I felt that I had made a real find. The hotel is just five minutes from the Plaza de las Tendillas and the same again from the Mezquita, much easier to find than some of the hotels hidden away in Cordoba's labyrinthine *Judería*. From the outside it looks much the same as any other town house. But within it stretches back via twin patios, each with a double tier of bedrooms. They are clean and inviting with wrought iron bedsteads, glass-topped bedside tables, white linen bed covers and sparkling bathrooms. The quietest are the ones in the far courtyard and their airconditioning, satellite TVs and internet access come as unexpected extras given the hotel's modest prices. A simple continental breakfast is served in a small breakfast room - which is also as clean as clean can be - or in the courtyard when weather permits. A reliable hotel for smaller budgets and when staying at Casa de los Naranjos guests can use the Hotel Afaros' car park for just €11 per day.

To see & do nearby: The Mezquita and the Jewish quarter, the Palace complex of Medina Azahara, walking in the Sierra Morena.

HOTEL CASA DE LOS AZULEJOS

Fernando Colón 5, 14002 Córdoba

Tel: 957 470 000 Fax: 957 475 496

Email: info@casadelosazulejos.com

www.casadelosazulejos.com

Management:	Manuel Luque Bendala
Closed:	December 24 & 25
Bedrooms:	8 Twin/Doubles
Prices:	Standard Double/Twin €85-120, Superior Double/Twin €100-140, Suite €120-170 + 7% VAT
Meals:	Breakfast included, Lunch/Dinner approx. €25. Restaurant closed Sunday night & Mondays.

Directions: Hotel is to the east of the Mezquita close to the Corredera square. Best to park in any central car park then take taxi or follow taxi to hotel which has 2 parking places.

Córdoba Province · Map 7 · HOTEL 099

Casa de los Azulejos is very much the reflection of its young owner, Manuel Luque Bendala. He studied at hotel school in Geneva then learned the ropes with a large hotel group in Mexico, whence the artistic inspiration for this small, zany hotel. His point of departure was an elegant town house which, in parts, is more than three centuries old. Stepping in to the brightly tiled courtyard – thus the hotel's name – you get a first taste of the hotel's cheery mood. There are masses of potted plants, interesting modern art, wacky tables and chairs and a hammock: the debt to the land of Zapata, Rivera and Kahlo is manifest in lamps (Mexican *sombreros*!), decorative ponchos, bright colours and, most notably, in its vaulted Guadalupana *cantina* restaurant. It leads straight out to the lively Corredera square and has a long mural depicting a traditional village folk scene. Here you can choose between 15 different *tequilas*, feast on traditional Mexican food ('not Tex-Mex!' insists Manuel) then climb the stairs to your bedroom whose décor, like that of the rest of the house, is lighthearted, stylish, colourful and amusing. Some readers have told me that ground floor rooms can be noisy so be sure to ask for '*una habitación tranquila*' should you book.

To see & do nearby: The Mezquita, the patios and gardens of the old town, the Sierra del Norte, Medina Azahara.

PALACIO DE BAILÍO

Calle Ramírez de las Casas Deza 10-12, 14001 Córdoba

Tel: 957 498 993 Fax: 957 498 994
Email: hospes.palaciodelbailio@hospes.es
www.hospes.es

Management:	Marta Águilar
Closed:	December 24 & 25
Bedrooms:	35 Superior Twin/Doubles, 10 Deluxe Twin/Doubles, 5 Junior Suites and 1 Grand Loft Suite
Prices:	Superior €175-210, Deluxe €195-230 Junior Suite €280-295, Grand Loft Suite €520-580 + 7% VAT
Meals:	Breakfast €18, Lunch/Dinner in Gastronomic Restaurant approx €45-60 or in tapas bar €20-25

Directions: From A4 follow signs 'Centro Ciudad'. Cross river and at roundabout exit along Paseo de la Victoria to the Duque de Rivas gardens. Here right to Plaza Colon then right into Calle Alfaros then follow signs.

Córdoba Province · Map 7 · HOTEL 100

This is, I admit, the odd man out in this guide book. A five star hotel, Bailio costs the double of most places listed here. I include it in the simple conviction that a night in Córdoba is an event to be celebrated and that this is a very fine place for a celebration. The series of buildings that make up the fabric of the hotel – it covers a 4.000 m^2 slice of the city's old centre – date back to the 16th century and were built on Roman foundations, still visible beneath the main patio's remarkable glass floor. Wandering through Bailio's gardens, courtyards and elegant salons is a truly sensual experience: here are frescos, finely carved ionic columns, vestiges of an old chapel, keyhole arches, intricate *mudéjar* ceilings as well as a decked pool overhung by palm and citrus trees. A multi-talented team of interior decorators have waved a magic wand over this narcotic backdrop, incorporating stunning contemporary lamps, mirrors, paintings and paint effects, and furnishings. Each of Bailio's bedrooms and suites is a remarkable work of art, with the same display of designer *derring-do*, and so too are the vaulted *tapas* bar and *Senzone* restaurant where Periko Ortega takes traditional cordoban cuisine to new places. And if you're really feeling like further indulgence, you can steam and soak, and then be massaged, in the hotel's *Bodyna* spa.

To see & do nearby: The old Jewish quarter, the Mezquita and Alcazar, the ruins at Medina Azahara, the Torre de la Calahorra museum.

LA HOSPEDERÍA DE EL CHURRASCO

Calle Romero 38, 14003 Córdoba

Tel: 957 294 808 Fax: 957 421 661
Email: hospederia@elchurrasco.com
www.elchurrasco.com

Management:	Juan Vicente Molinas Jurado
Closed:	Never
Bedrooms:	6 Standard Twin/Doubles and 3 Superior Doubles
Prices:	Standard Double/Twin €130-150, Superior Double €170-190 + 7% VAT
Meals:	Breakfast included, no other meals but excellent food at sister restaurant next door, approx. €30-35, closed August.

Directions: From Sevilla exit from A4/E5 for Centro Cuidad. Cross river then at r'bout take first exit along Paseo de la Victoria. Park in Aparcamiento Paseo de la Victoria (hotel guests get reduced rate of €15). Hotel at end of Calle Romero approx. 100m northwest of Mezquita.

Córdoba Province · Map 7 · HOTEL 101

35 years have passed since Rafael Carrillo opened the El Churrasco restaurant and the place has long since earned its place in the culinary history of the city. And bless the day that his family decided to branch out and open a small hotel in an ancient *Judería* mansion house, just a few yards along the street from the eatery. This is the pristine, coquettish small hotel that the city has always lacked and goes straight to the top of my 'where to stay in Cordoba' list. You enter through a fine wafer-bricked entrance which opens out onto a typical *patio cordobés* whose centrepiece is the house's original well. Just beyond is a second, smaller patio with glass-topped tables where you breakfast to the sound of a trickling fountain and, off to one side, a cosy little bar where you can kick off your evening with a chilled glass of *montilla*. Nine sumptuous, festive bedrooms complete the picture. They are decorated in a mix of plain pastels and stripes with shining floors of polished parquet and richly patterned curtain and bed fabrics. They come with the full quotient of extras like sat TV, minibar, even a computer, with a hydromassage tub and monogrammed towels awaiting you in the bathroom. And when it comes to deciding on where to have dinner, well, there's only really one choice.

To see & do nearby: The Mezquita and the Jewish Quarter, the palace complex of Medina Azahara, walking in the Sierra Morena.

HOTEL ZUHAYRA

Calle Mirador 10, 14870 Zuheros

Tel: 957 694 693 Fax: 957 694 702

Email: hotelzuhayra@zercahoteles.com

www.zercahoteles.com

Management:	José & Antonio Ábalos Guerrero
Closed:	June 23 – July 16
Bedrooms:	5 Doubles and 13 Twins
Prices:	Double/Twin €51-64 + 7% VAT
Meals:	Breakfast included, Lunch/Dinner €12 set menu or €18-25 à la carte, excluding wine.

Directions: From Málaga north towards Córdoba on the A45/N331 to Lucena. Here turn right and follow A-339 to Cabra then on towards Doña Mencía on A-318 then turn right to Zuheros. Leave car in car park by castle. Hotel on right as you go down Calle Mirador.

Córdoba Province · Map 7 · HOTEL 102

Zuheros has been spared the tourist onslaught because of its remote location. Yet this is one of Andalucía's most spectacular villages with whitewashed houses clinging to an outcrop of limestone rock, topped by a high castle: the quintessential Romantic vision of southern Spain. If you make the detour be sure to stay at Hotel Zuhayra. From the outside it's a rather unexciting edifice but thanks to its lofty location all of its rooms are blessed with great views out across the town. They are sparklingly clean with simple pine furniture and with bright fabrics for bedspreads and curtains adding a twist of colour. I liked their sober, uncluttered feel and they are really well equipped given the price. On the ground floor there's a slightly dark, cavernous bar area but far nicer in feel is the cosy first floor restaurant where the menu looks to the best of traditional, Andalusian country cuisine. Specialities include *salmorejo* (a thick gazpacho), *remojón* (made with hake and oranges), aubergines cooked with honey and some interesting salad variations, a rare find in this part of the world. The two brothers who run the hotel are exceptionally friendly and there are wonderful walks leading out from the village: you may just coincide with walking groups from England who for years have used this trustworthy hotel as a base for their rambles.

To see & do nearby: Walking in the Subbética Park, La Cueva de los Murcielagos (the cave of the bats), the castle and museum of Zuheros.

HUERTA DE LAS PALOMAS

Ctra Priego-Zagrilla km 3,5, 14800 Priego de Córdoba

Tel: 957 720 305/393 Fax: 957 720 007
Email: huertadelaspalomas@zercahoteles.com
www.zercahoteles.com

Management:	Salvador Ábalos Guerrero
Closed:	January 7 – February 7
Bedrooms:	16 Standard Twin/Doubles, 14 Superior Twin/Doubles, 2 Junior Suites and 2 Suites
Prices:	Standard Double/Twin €81-97, Superior Double/Twin €90-105, Junior Suite €115-135, Suite €135-155 + 7% VAT
Meals:	Breakfast included, Lunch/Dinner €18 (menu) or approx. €30-3 à la carte.

Directions: From Málaga towards Córdoba on A45/N331 to Lucena. Here turn right and follow A339 to Cabra then on towards Priego de Córdoba. Just before Priego turn left for Zagrilla on CO82111 and follow signs to hotel.

Zagrilla? The chances are you may not have heard of this pretty little hamlet and maybe not even of Priego, one of many unsung Andalusian jewels that remain well off the tourist-beaten track. The owners of the Huerta believe that the place has a future and cut no corners when creating this luxurious and unmistakably southern hotel. The entrance hall strikes a merry note with bright ceramic tiles and its festive blue and yellow colour scheme. From here a broad staircase leads through to a triple-tiered patio with light flooding in from lofty skylights and lit at night by two enormous chandeliers. Bedrooms, each named after a village in the area and with photographs to match, are supremely comfortable. All of them have minibars, internet connections and swish bathrooms with double sinks, most with both bath and separate shower. The hotel's restaurant tries hard on both decorative and gastronomic levels: 'traditional recipes with an *avante garde*-ish touch' was how Salvador described the cuisine, recommending his *remojón* (made with hake and oranges) and a mixed entrée, *Las delicias del Califa*. In the lawned gardens is a huge pool, there's a tennis club next door and the old centre of Priego, with its extraordinary *Fuente del Rey*, is just ten minutes drive away.

To see & do nearby: The old centre of Priego, Zagrilla Alta, the Roman ruins at Almedinilla, day trips to Córdoba and Granada.

HOTELS 104 – 121

GRANADA

HOTEL LA ENREA

Paraje de la Enrea s/n, 18270 Montefrío

Tel: 958 336 662 Fax: 958 336 796

Email: hotellaenrea@zercahoteles.com

www.zercahoteles.com

Management:	Jorge Delgado
Closed:	January 7 – February 7
Bedrooms:	17 Twin/Doubles and 1 Special Double
Prices:	Double/Twin €51-64, Special Double €72-84 + 7% VAT
Meals:	Breakfast included, Lunch/Dinner €13 (set menu) or approx. €20-25 à la carte including wine.

Directions: From Málaga A45 towards Granada/Córdoba and then A92 towards Granada. Exit for Huetor-Tajar then follow signs to Montefrío. Here head towards Tocón. Hotel signposted.

Granada Province · Map 8 · HOTEL 104

Montefrío remains, most blessedly, another of Andalucía's undiscovered jewels. Approaching through the mountains to the south you round a bend in the serpentine road to see, up ahead in the distance, one of the most spectacular villages of the South. Narrow streets of whitewashed houses spill out beneath a jagged face of rock which is topped by a 16th century church and a walled, Moorish *alcazaba*. To one side of the village a gorge of deeply weathered sandstone cuts south from the village to end, by an ancient cross, at the doors of La Enrea. It has recently been taken under the sheltering wing of the Abalos brothers who also manage the Zuhayra and Huerta de las Palomas, both listed in this guide. With these kind folk at the helm things can only be good. The decorative style throughout the hotel is umistakably southern: marble floors, framed floral prints, a few potted plants. Nothing remotely *chic* but the bedrooms are clean, comfortable and exceptionally good value. And the food follows the same cue. All of the region's traditional dishes are on the menu: try the *lomo en orza* (loin of pork preserved in olive oil), perhaps with *salmorejo* or *gazpacho* as a starter. And there's great walking straight out from the hotel and Montefrío to explore where you probably won't hear anything apart from Spanish being spoken.

To see & do nearby: The old centre of Montefrío, dolmens at La Peña de los Gitanos, Granada and the Alhambra.

CORTIJO LA FE

Solana de Covaleda, 18270 Granada

Tel: 639 721 740 or 958 348 763 Fax: 958 348 167

Email: info@cortijolafe.com

www.cortijolafe.com

Management:	Dominque Boureau & Richard Le Forban
Closed:	Rarely
Bedrooms:	4 Doubles, 2 Triples and 1 Suite for 4
Prices:	Double/Twin €83-105, Triple €96-115, Suite for 4 €175 including VAT. Rental of complete cortijo €640 daily.

Directions: From Málaga head north towards Granada on the A45 then east on A92-M then A92. Leave A92 at exit 206 for Villanueva de Mesía. Arriving in Tocón turn left at a small petrol station towards Montefrío. Continue for 8.1 kilometers to Cortijo 'La Chopa'. Here turn left and follow signs for 2 kilometers to Cortijo La Fe.

Granada Province · Map 8 · HOTEL 105

When Dominique and Richard decided to leave France in search of a Shangri-La in the South they had no desire to rush. After an odyssey of more than 20,000 kilometers – it took them to Andalucía's furthest flung corners – a chance encounter with a local farmer and an evening of shared conversation lead them to La Fe. It's easy to see why the place worked its magic on them. The farm sits alone on an isolated bluff with soaring views across groves of olive and almond to the distant mountains. After months of restoration, and several more of creation, they have reborn the farm and it breathes a wholesome and deeply relaxing ethic. The eight bedrooms take the area's Moorish legacy as their touchstone and strike a perfect balance between simple good looks and solid comfort. They are beamed with terracotta floors, attractive shower rooms and most have open hearths as well as really effective central heating. And wrapped into the fabric of La Fe is a colourful Moroccan sitting room, an amazing *hammam* as well as a small chapel with a series of inspirational contemporary murals. Cortijo La Fe, as the name implies, lifts you well above the everyday and is a treat for all five senses.

To see & do nearby: Granada and the Alhambra and Albayzín, walks out from the farm, la Peña de los Gitanos, reading, writing and painting at La Fe.

LA SEGUIRIYA

Calle Peñas 12, 18120 Alhama de Granada

Tel: 958 360 801 or 625 102 110 Fax: 958 360 915
Email: laseguiriya@laseguiriya.com
www.laseguiriya.com

Management:	Paco Moyano & Lola Maiztegui
Closed:	Never
Bedrooms:	1 Single, 3 Doubles, 1 Family Room and 1 Suite
Prices:	Single €40, Double €60, Family Room €90, Suite €90 + 7% VAT
Meals:	Breakfast included, Lunch/Dinner approx. €30 including wine. Restaurant closed on Thursday and Sunday evening.

Directions: From Málaga A7/E15 towards Motril. Exit for Vélez Málaga. Bypass the town and after approx. 10 kms bear right on A335 to Alhama de Granada. Here follow signs for 'Ayuntamiento' then for hotel. Best to park in Plaza de la Constitución.

If you're an *aficionado* of flamenco you may recognise the name Paco Moyano. Before retiring from the life of itinerant artist Paco travelled to many different countries with his group of musicians and dancers. Flamenco is still a part of his life and if you stay at La Seguiriyá expect to hear some of the finest cante around, albeit on tape or CD (very occasionally *en directo* in winter). Paco and his wife Lola have made the transition with natural ease from musical artistry to that required to run their small village inn which nudges right up to the edge of the spectacular Alhama gorge. They've created a real home-from-home and the series of rooms which make up this deliciously cosy inn have nothing to do with corporate hospitality. Ceilings are are low and beamed and there is an eclectic collection of contemporary paintings, some of them the work of Paco's daughter Elvira. Lola is a really good cook and makes interesting salads, too, whilst Paco is front-of-house, always finding time to share experiences of life, and of his art, with guests. Heed his recommendations when it comes to choosing your wine and find time to visit the hot springs which well up just outside of the village, reached by way of a dramatic, rocky defile..

To see & do nearby: The old arab quarter of Alhama, the spa, the footpath of Los Angeles, day trips to Granada.

LA TARTANA

Urbanización San Nicolás, 18697 La Herradura

Tel: 958 640 535 Fax: 958 640 535

Email: reservations@hotellatartana.com

www.hotellatartana.com

Management:	Penny Jarret, Barry Branham & Joachim Holter
Closed:	Mid January – early February
Bedrooms:	4 Doubles and 4 Twins
Prices:	Double/Twin €57-87 + 7% VAT
Meals:	Breakfast included, Dinner €25-30 excluding wine

Directions: From Málaga A7/E15/N340 east towards Motril. Exit for la Herradura. Don't go in to village but rather make U turn at traffic lights then head back towards Málaga for just 100 metres then take first right into Urbanización San Nicolás. Hotel is first building on left.

Granada Province · Map 8 · HOTEL 107

La Tartana is one of this part of the coast's oldest guest houses but recently saw a complete metamorphosis thanks to the combined *savoir faire* of Penny, Barry and Joachim. The hotel is just back from the busy N340 but although you can hear the traffic it hardly detracts from the place's high feel-good factor. The garden is wonderful, there are views out to the sparkling ocean and as guest here you are made to feel really special: your hosts have been in the hospitality business for years. The bedrooms, all of which have been recently redecorated, look on to a balconied, central patio with a rambling creeper and a pretty sandstone fountain. But what lifts the place into the special category is the colourful restaurant. If you're tiring of the normal *andaluz* fare then Joachim's cuisine, which takes it's key from the recipe books of America, Thailand and Mexico, will come as a a welcome change. Ingredients are always fresh, flavours inspired and the pastry truly exceptional. La Tartana is an easy drive from the airport, there are good beaches close by and Granada is an easy day trip from La Herredura.

To see & do nearby: Beaches and water sports, hiking in the Sierra Nevada, day trips to Granada.

EL CORTIJO DEL PINO

Fernán Nuñez 2, La Loma, 18659 Albuñuelas

Tel: 958 776 257 or 607 523 767 Fax: 958 776 350

Email: cortijodelpino@gmail.com

www.elcortijodelpinolecrin.com

Management:	Antonia Ruano & James Connel
Closed:	Never
Bedrooms:	1 Single, 1 Double, 3 Twins or complete house can be rented throughout the year
Prices:	Single €65, Double/Twin €85-110 or complete house €1500-2000 weekly including VAT
Meals:	Breakfast included, no other meals. 2 local restaurants

Directions: From Málaga to Granada on A45, then A359, then A92. Just before Granada branch onto A323 motorway towards Motril then take exit 153 for Albuñuelas. Here as you arrive in village turn right by a bus stop. A steep road leads you up to El Cortijo del Pino.

You spot the massive Aleppo pine tree that towers above Cortijo del Pino and gives the house its names from miles away. It stands guardian to the old farmhouse that this Anglo-Spanish couple turned into one of Andalucía's most attractive small B&Bs. They run it in the very best tradition of *mi casa es tu casa* (my home is your home). James is an artist and sometimes gives courses at the house (details on request). And there would be plenty to inspire you, whether you were attempting a still life or a landscape. Every corner of the house has been decorated and arranged with an artist's sensitivity and the views across the wooded valley to Albuñuelas are simply magnificent. The four doubles are big on space and all of them have been beautifully decorated by Antonia with her family heirlooms, huge beds, beautiful tiles and taps, hand-embroidered curtains, excellent bathrooms and James' paintings. I have the fondest memories of awaking to the sound of birdsong and the chiming of the church bells across the valley, of a delightful stay in the very best of company. An added bonus is that the swimming pool is heated throughout the year, even more reason for getting a group of friends together and renting the whole house for a week.

To see & do nearby: The Alhambra, the villages of La Alpujarra, the Costa Tropical and the Lecrín Valley.

HOTEL AMERICA

Real de La Alhambra 53, 18009 Granada

Tel: 958 227 471 Fax: 958 227 470

Email: reservas@hotelamericagranada.com

www.hotelamericagranada.com

Management:	Maribel Alconchel
Closed:	Never
Bedrooms:	4 Singles, 5 Doubles, 7 Twins and 1 Suite
Prices:	Single €70, Double/Twin €115, Suite €140 including VAT
Meals:	Breakfast €8 (included in July/August), simple Lunches €17 excluding wine. Restaurant closed at weekends.

Directions: Round Granada following signs for Alhambra/Sierra Nevada on the 'Ronda Sur' ring road. Up the hill towards the Alhambra then follow signs to hotel making sure to keep to the left so as not to enter car parks. Leave baggage at hotel then leave car in one of the Alhambra car parks.

Granada Province · Map 8 · HOTEL 109

For years and years Hotel America has been one of the very best places to stay in Granada. There's only one problem. Unless you book weeks ahead the chances are that it will be full. The reason for its popularity is not only that it is an immensely attractive hotel just yards from the Alhambra but also because of the good, old-fashioned hospitality of the Alonchel family. Three generations of them have managed the America since it opened its doors in 1936 (the place began its life as the summer residence of a well-to-do Duchess). Guests invariably gravitate towards the plant-filled courtyard which doubles as the hotel's restaurant. Here sparrows hop between ceramic-topped tables and a Virginia creeper and rambling ivy help keep the sun at bay. It can get busy at lunchtime and is best enjoyed later in the day when the coach parties are heading back down the hill. I'd try to book a bedroom on the top floor (numbers 212 or 214) which have recently been completely redecorated in a warm, sponged ochre tones and which feel as welcoming as the rest of the hotel. And what a privilege to be able to wander straight out from the hotel and, in seconds, be at the main entrance to the Alhambra.

To see & do nearby: The Alhambra and Sacromonte, the Carthusian monastery of La Cartuja, the Albayzín area.

HOTEL CASA MORISCA

Cuesta de la Victoria 9, 18010 Granada

Tel: 958 221 100 Fax: 958 215 796

Email: info@hotelcasamorisca.com

www.hotelcasamorisca.com

Management:	María Jesús Candenas & Carlos Sánchez
Closed:	Never
Bedrooms:	5 Doubles, 8 Twins and 1 Suite
Prices:	Double/Twin €118-148, Suite €198 + 7% VAT
Meals:	Breakfast €12, no Lunch/Dinner available. Huge choice of restaurants and tapas bars within walking distance.

Directions: From the Plaza Nueva follow Acera del Darro almost to the end (the Alhambra will be to your right) and the Cuesta de La Victoria is last-but-one turning to the left. Or, much simpler, park anywhere in centre and take taxi to hotel.

Granada Province · Map 8 · HOTEL 110

The Casa Morisca is amongst a number of Albayzín mansion houses which have been transformed into a small hotels. This is a very old house: the owners have documents tracing its origins back to the end of the 15th century. As its name suggests, the architecture of the house is that beloved of the Moors, a style that continued to be prevalent long after their expulsion. Here are wafer brick columns, delicate keyhole arches, polychromatic tiles with Arabic calligraphy and the most amazing of *mudéjar* wooden ceilings. This is the perfect place to prolong that Alhambra moment and from many of the fourteen bedrooms you look straight out to the Comares tower. All have been decorated with warmth and style: there are intricate Alhambra-style moldings, bright kilims, pastel colours and fabulous bathrooms. The lighting is subtle, beds superb and the place is surprisingly quiet given the city centre location. You breakfast in a barrel-vaulted dining room to the murmur of the courtyard fountain. And when it comes to lunch or dinner you are spoilt for choice: you are yards from the lively Acera del Darro with its many terrace bars and restaurants which look up to the Torre de la Vela. And the hotel's staff are amongst the friendliest, most helpful that I've come across.

To see & do nearby: Sacromonte and the Abadía, the Albayzín area and the Acera del Darro (great tapas bars).

CASA DEL CAPITEL NAZARÍ

Cuesta Aceituneros 6, Albayzín-Plaza Nueva, 18010 Granada

Tel: 958 215 260 Fax: 958 215 806

Email: info@hotelcasacapitel.com

www.hotelcasacapitel.com

Management:	Angela Caracuel Vera
Closed:	Never
Bedrooms:	10 Doubles and 7 Twins
Prices:	Double/Twin €72-99, Double/Twin with Alhambra View €84-111 + 7% VAT
Meals:	Breakfast €8

Directions: Best to park in parking Plaza Puerta Real in the centre of Granada. Take taxi from rank immediately outside and hotel will refund cost of taxi.

Granada Province · Map 8 · HOTEL 111

The Darro gorge cuts a deep cleft through Granada's old centre. From its northern bank the narrow streets of the Albayzín quarter cut anarchically upwards, a plexus of narrow alleyways with an architectural delight around every corner. Since being declared a *Unesco World Heritage* site the area has seen huge changes, including the opening of a number of small hotels. The Casa del Capitel is amongst the best of them and is excellent value given its location and degree of comfort. The bedrooms are reached by way of a columned and balconied courtyard. They are smallish but feel snug rather than stifling and have warm colour washes, wooden ceilings, *retro* taps, nice lamps and all the add-ons like airconditioning, TVs, telephones, wifi and mini bars. The building is a fascinating potpourri of architectural elements; a *Renaissance palacete* (grand town house) with Roman columns, a Moorish capital atop one of its ancient columns (from whence the name) and magnificent polychromatic *mudéjar* geometric ceilings whose restoration took more than three years. The nicest room is number 22 which has a 16th century carved ceiling and view of the crenelated walls of the Alhambra. And the staff are delightful.

To see & do nearby: The Alhambra, the Cathedral and Royal chapel, exploring the narrow streets of the Albayzín.

CASA DEL ALJARIFE

Placeta de la Cruz Verde 2, 18010 Granada

Tel: 958 222 425 Fax: 958 222 425

Email: cdagranada@yahoo.es

www.casadelaljarife.com

Management:	María del Carmen López García & Christian Most
Closed:	August 15–30
Bedrooms:	1 Double, 2 Twins and 1 Suite for 4
Prices:	Double/Twin €91, Suite €168 + 7% VAT
Meals:	Breakfast €5, Lunch/Dinner only tapas available. Many excellent restaurants close to Aljarife.

Directions: Park in any city centre car park – the nearest is Aparcamiento de San Agustín – then walk to the Plaza Nueva. Ring Christian who will come down and guide you to the Casa del Aljarife.

Granada Province · Map 8 · HOTEL 112

The Albayzín should always be your first choice when choosing where to spend a night in Granada. Strung out along the Darro gorge there are masses of lively bars and restaurants, the views across to the Alhambra are enchanting and its plexus of narrow alleyways speaks of a different age. Christian and María del Carmen had already bought and restored this grand 17th century house long before the area became *the* place to live in Granada. Like so many of the Albayzín's houses, the façade gives little away but once you pass through the heavy wooden doors you emerge into a huge cobbled courtyard where a deliciously rambling garden of laurel, jasmine, aspidistra and bougainvillaea evoke passages from The Arabian Nights. This is the place where you'll inevitably spend most of your time, but the bedrooms, too, are really comfortable: airconditioned for the summer, centrally heated for the winter, a couple grab a view of the Alhambra. Christian is a really cheery host and has thoughtfully put together his own listing of the best bars and restaurants in town and the visiting times for Granada's most interesting monuments.

To see & do nearby: The Albayzín, the Alhambra, concerts in the Manuel de Falla concert hall, the Carthusian monastery of La Cartuja.

MIGUELETES

Calle Benalúa 11, Plaza Nueva, 18010 Granada

Tel: 958 210 700 Fax: 958 210 702

Email: migueletes@room-matehotels.com

www.room-matehotels.com

Management:	Ana Raczkowski
Closed:	Last 3 weeks in January
Bedrooms:	23 Doubles/Twins and 2 Suites
Prices:	Standard Double/Twin €80-140, Executive Double/Twin €120-180, Junior Suite €150-220, Alhambra Suite €220-330 + 7% VAT
Meals:	Breakfast included, no other meals but several restaurants very close.

Directions: From A44 ring road take exit 129 for Centro/Recogidas. Head in to centre and leave car at Parking Plaza Puerta Real then taxi to hotel. Keep receipt: it will be deducted from your bill.

Granada Province · Map 8 · HOTEL 113

The Darro gorge cuts a deep gash through the Sierra de Nevada's westernmost flank. To one side the fortifications of the Alhambra reach skywards whilst to the other the Albayzín, the oldest quarter of the city, climbs up a steep hillside, peppered with some of Granada's finest town houses. Migueletes has seen almost four centuries of habitation and takes its name from the police division who were billeted here and whose brief was to bring the last of the *bandoleros* to justice. In its more recent history the hotel has been taken under the wing of the quirky Room Mate group which aims to imbue all of their hotels with the personality of its imaginary owners, in this case the Miguelete brothers: young, urbane and artistic! The bedrooms are as good as any in the city and a couple have views across to the Alhambra. Beds are enormous, bedding superb and traditional floors of highly polished terracotta and intricate *mudéjar* woodwork evoke the cultural melting pot that once was Granada. Nothing is too much trouble for Migueletes' staff who are young and relaxed: they'll buy your Alhambra tickets, advise on where best to eat and steer you towards the best of what's on the cultural agenda. An elegant galleried mansion at the heart of old Granada, this hotel ranks high on my list of favourites.

To see & do nearby: The Alhambra, the Cathedral and the Carthusian monastery of La Cartuja, day trips to the Sierra Nevada and Alpujarras.

HOTEL SANTA ISABEL LA REAL

Calle Santa Isabel La Real 17&19, Albayzín, 18010 Granada

Tel: 958 294 658 Fax: 958 294 645

Email: info@hotelsantaisabellareal.com

www.hotelsantaisabellareal.com

Management:	Elena, Lola and Rafael del Castrillo
Closed:	August 1–31
Bedrooms:	2 Standard Doubles, 3 Special Doubles, 5 Superior Doubles and 1 Tower Junior Suite
Prices:	Standard Double €80-100, Special Double €100-120, Superior Double €120-140, Tower Junior Suite €150-170 + 7% VAT
Meals:	Breakfast €10, snacks available at other times of day.

Directions: Park in Aparcamiento San Agustín or El Triunfo (guests have reduced rates) then taxi to hotel. Hotel also has 5 spaces in an adjacent car park @ €12 daily but call for arrival instructions.

Granada Province · Map 8 · HOTEL 114

A plethora of boutique hotels have sprung up on the Albayzín hill over the past few years but few are as big on charm and comfort as Santa Isabel la Real. The hotel stands cheek by jowl with the monastery of the same name and is just yards from the square of San Miguel Bajo, one of the best places in the city for *al fresco* meals. The Castrillo family found this former *casa de vecinos* in a state of advanced decay but managed restoration in such a way that large parts of the existing edifice were preserved along with the flavour of *Times Past* in its columned and balconied *patio granadino*. Brother and sisters Rafael, Elena and Lola were entrusted with decorating and furnishing the 9 bedrooms and have infused them with warmth and colour: bright rugs, rich tapestries as bed heads and an appealing mix of antique furnishing with top spec mod cons. The rooms are on three floors and a couple grab views of the Alhambra, the best being those from the romantic Tower Suite. And breakfast, like your room, is just the thing: fresh orange or lemon juice to put a zing in your step, homemade cakes and jams, cheeses and ham, *tostadas* and coffee. A regular minibus passes right by the hotel which will whisk you up to the Alhambra hill in minutes and, if you call ahead, the hotel will arrange your tickets for you. How's that for service?

To see & do nearby: The Alhambra, the Carthusian monastery of La Cartuja, the Sacromonte Caves, the Albayzín area.

CASA RURAL LA SEVILLANA

Calle Carretera 3, 18412 Bubión

Tel: 958 763 153 or 628 132 357
Email: casalasevillana@hotmail.com
www.casalasevillana.es

Management:	Eva Love & Julio Remón
Closed:	Never
Bedrooms:	1 Single, 3 Doubles and 3 Twins
Prices:	Single €35, Double/Twin €55 including VAT
Meals:	Breakfast included. Several restaurants a short walk away.

Directions: From Málaga A7/E15/N340 towards Motril then towards Granada on A44/E902. Exit for Vélez de Benaudalla then follow signs for Órgiva. Go through village then turn right by garage on GR421. Go through Pampaneira towards Pitres then turn left up hill to Bubion. House next to Teide restaurant.

Bubión is one of the Alpujarras' most dramatic villages, clinging to the edge of a steep-sided *barranco*, a dizzy 1350 metres above sea level, with vast views southwards towards the sea. The natural generosity of its people is reflected in their *tapas* culture: have a few beers or glasses of wine here and you'll have eaten the equivalent of a full meal. Casa Rural La Sevillana is to one side of the road which cuts up through the village towards Capileira and once belonged to the local electricity company. Eva and Julio have long been involved in organising holidays in the area. It seemed a natural step for them to set up their own village inn, aiming to provide simple comfort to the many people who come to walk and ride in the area. The rooms aren't enormous and have, for the most part, small shower rooms. They are simply furnished with Indian artifacts and hangings adding a twist of spice and colour. Beyond the cosy lounge, where a log fire burns in the colder months, is a leafy courtyard where you are served a generous breakfast when weather permits. Few people know this area as well as your hosts and Eva's sister, Dallas Love, organises day and week long riding trips. For more details see www.horse-riding.com.

To see & do nearby: Walking and riding in the Alpujarra, the Buddhist monastery, day trips to Granada.

HOTEL TARAY BOTÁNICO

Ctra A-348 Km 18, 18400 Órgiva

Tel: 958 784 525 Fax: 958 784 531

Email: tarayalp@teleline.es

www.hoteltaray.com

Management:	María Angela González
Closed:	January 10–20
Bedrooms:	9 Doubles, 3 Suites and 2 Suites with private terrace
Prices:	Double €83, Suite €112, Suite with terrace €115 including VAT
Meals:	Breakfast €7, Lunch/Dinner €14

Directions: From Granada A44 south towards Motril then exit on A348 to Lanjarón. Here continue to Órgiva. Straight into village then bear sharp right following signs for Torvizcón/Cadiar. The hotel is signposted to the left as you leave Órgiva, just before you reach the river.

Granada Province · Map 8 · HOTEL 116

Órgiva has had a lot of press, mostly good and occasionally bad, since it began attracting northern European travellers in search of new pastures for their tipis, benders and vans. The pace of life here is a gentle one and parts of the valley have an almost sub-tropical air: saddled between the Sierra Nevada and Contraviesa range the climate is much milder than in the high Alpujarran villages. Everything grows with such gusto that a decade after planting out gardens and orchards, and opening what was plain 'Hotel Taray', its owners decided to add the 'botanico' epithet. But if the 15.000 square metres of orchards, lawns and organic veggies are the Taray's joy, the rest of the hotel is pretty pukka too. The bungalow-style bedrooms stretch away from the main building and have been prettily decorated with locally woven bedspreads and curtains which are nicely in synch with beamed roofs and terracotta floors. The same trad-rustic style is on show in the twin dining rooms which feel especially snug in winter when the log fires are burning. Taray's menu sticks mostly to local recipes like thick stews and game, there's a reasonably priced wine list and you're treated to the same friendly service that greets you in reception. This is a small hotel with a generous ethic and is deservedly popular amongst the walking community.

To see & do nearby: Walking in the Alpujarra, day trips to Granada and the coast, exploring Europe's highest villages and ascents of mainland Spain's highest mountain.

SIERRA Y MAR

Calle Albaycín 3, 18414 Ferreirola

Tel: 958 766 171 Fax: 958 857 367

Email: sierraymar@hotmail.com

www.sierraymar.com

Management:	Inger Norgaard & Giuseppe Heiss
Closed:	January
Bedrooms:	2 Singles, 7 Twin/Doubles and 1 Triple
Prices:	Single €36, Double/Twin €56, Triple €76 including VAT
Meals:	Breakfast included, no other meals. Restaurant a 10 minute walk from Sierra y Mar in Fondales.

Directions: From Málaga A7/E15/N340 towards Motril then towards Granada on A44/E902. Exit for Vélez de Benaudalla then follow signs for Órgiva. Go through village then turn right by garage on GR421. Go through Pampaneira and just before Pitres turn right to Mecina. Through village to Ferreirola: park in square and walk 100 metres to house.

Jose and Inger have run this simple B&B for several years and were amongst the first foreigners to settle in this part of the Alpujarra. They chose the tiniest of hamlets, Ferreirola, where donkeys still outnumbered cars and where there would be no chance of being disturbed by passing traffic. The road ends in the square and you walk the final fifty yards to Sierra y Mar's cheerful blue entrance. It leads to a shady, walled garden where time seems to slow down a pace or two. The emphasis here is on the simple, the homespun, the wholesome and the authentic. Bedrooms have no chain hotel extras but are all clean, comfortable and quiet. Most are in the main house where there's a guest lounge with masses of documentation on walking: few people know the mountains round here like José who has worked as a mountain guide for many years. There's a wonderful circular walk straight out from the house and although only breakfast is available, just ten minute's walk from the house is one of the area's most characterful restaurants. There's also a great vegetarian restaurant just up the road or you're welcome to make use of the kitchen to prepare your own food.

To see & do nearby: Walking and riding, the Roman bridge in Fondales, the nearby villages of Las Alpujarras.

HOTEL LA FRAGUA

Calle San Antonio 4, 18417 Trevélez

Tel: 958 858 626 or 958 858 512 Fax: 958 858 614
Email: reservas@hotellafragua.com
www.hotellafragua.com

Management:	Antonio & Miguel Espinosa
Closed:	January 7 – February 10
Bedrooms:	4 Singles, 4 Doubles, 6 Twins and 10 Twin/Doubles with terraces
Prices:	Single €30, Double/Twin €40, Double/Twin with terrace €40, Double/Twin in La Fragua II €50 + 7% VAT
Meals:	Breakfast €4, Lunch/Dinner approx. €15 including wine

Directions: From Granada A44 south towards Motril then exit on C333. Go through Lanjarón and just before Órgiva turn left to Trevélez. Here go steeply up hill to the 'barrio medio' and park near to La Plaza de las Pulgas. La Fragua is next to the 'Ayuntamiento' (town hall).

Granada Province · Map 8 · HOTEL 118

Trevélez is one of the better-known villages in la Alpujarra, a favourite with the weekend-in-the-country crowd and a popular base for the walking community. From here you can climb the Sierra Nevada's highest peak, the Mulhacén (you'll be starting at a height of nearly 1500m!) and the GR7 long distance footpath loops past the village. La Fragua is one of the village's highest buildings and has an amazing vista of the valley and the distant Contraviesa Sierra. The bedrooms are simple, no nonsense affairs but they are quiet and clean and the nicest of them have their own terraces. Breakfasts and other meals are served at the sister restaurant of the same name which is just 50 metres down the street. It has a cosy pine-clad dining room hoisted above the bar: windows to three sides catch that same wonderful view out across the village. La Fragua's menu focuses on things traditional. Try the spicy lamb (*cordero a la moruña*), the partridge (*perdíz del cura a la antigua*) or the generously priced set menu. And a sister hotel, La Fragua II, has recently been completed with larger rooms, great views and it is well worth the extra few euros. It is also just a shake away from the restaurant.

To see & do nearby: Visit to a secadero to see how cured hams are prepared, trout-fishing in the Río Trevélez (early May to early September) and walking.

EL PARAJE

Ctra Granada – Berchules A-4130 km 24, 18451 Bérchules

Tel: 958 064 029 or 626 186 035

Email: info@elparaje.com

www.elparaje.com

Management:	Anita Beijer & Walter Michels
Closed:	Rarely
Bedrooms:	2 Doubles, 2 Twins and 1 Apartment
Prices:	Double/Twin €45, Apartment sleeping 2 or 3 €55 including VAT
Meals:	Breakfast €3.50, Dinner €15 excluding wine

Directions: From Málaga A7/E15 then N340 towards Almería. Pass Motril then exit for Albuñol. Bypass village then right on GR433 to Cadiar then on towards Mecina. At junction left to Bérchules and at next junction left towards Juviles (don't enter Bérchules!). Continue for 2 kms then turn right at sign for El Paraje.

Granada Province · Map 8 · HOTEL 119

Anita and Walter, nurturing a dream of running a small inn in southern Spain, happened on this ancient farm in 2001 and knew they'd found the place. And what a position, right beside the GR7 long distance path, 1400 metres up on the Sierra Nevada's southern flank with soaring views south towards the Contraviesa mountains. They've created a house of human proportions which radiates wholesome energy: don't expect hotelly luxury but rather simple, homespun rooms whose almost monastic feel is in synch with El Paraje's guiding ethic. And food, like your room, is exceptionally good value. Walter is in charge of the culinary side of things and, whilst acknowledging a debt to the 'Moro' cookbook as well as to French and Dutch influences, he says that he is 'more triggered by the season than by books'. Herbs and some of the veg come straight from an organic garden and dinners are a doubly special occasion when you eat beneath stars on the old *era* that cuts an arc in front of the house. You'll hear a resident owl at night and wake to a symphony of songbirds. This is a place to stay for at least two or three nights and put time aside to hike out into the mountains. Anita and Walter have a number of walking routes mapped out and will advise on which ones to choose, according to the season and your abilities.

To see & do nearby: Mountain biking, walking the long distance GR7 footpath (it runs past the house), riding.

ALQUERÍA DE MORAYMA

A-348 Cádiar–Torvizcón km 52, 18440 Cádiar

Tel: 958 343 221 or 958 343 303 Fax: 958 343 221
Email: alqueria@alqueriamorayma.com
www.alqueriamorayma.com

Management:	Mariano Cruz Fajardo
Closed:	Never
Bedrooms:	3 Doubles, 15 Twins, 1 Suite and 3 Apartments
Prices:	Double/Twin €66, Suite €69, Apartment for 4 €98 + 7% VAT
Meals:	Breakfast €3, Lunch/Dinner €12 including wine

Directions: From Granada A44 south towards Motril then exit on A348 to Lanjarón. Here continue to Órgiva and Torvizcón and on towards Cádiar on A-348. La Alquería de Morayma is 2 kms before Cádiar, at km 52, to the left of the road.

The Alquería de Morayma lies just east of the deep *barranco* that author Chris Stewart put on the map in his best-selling *Driving Over Lemons*. This is fantastic walking country and the long distance footpath that winds its way across the Alpujarra passes just yards from Morayma. Mariano Cruz wanted to create something more than a place to sleep and eat at La Alquería. He encourages his guests to actually immerse themselves in the traditional way of life of the area. So you can join in with the harvest and the milling of the farm's olives, help to make goat's cheese, harvest his grapes or even take part in the winter *matanza* (the slaughter and preparation of a pig). The rooms and houses have been conceived with the idea of re-creating the ambience of one of the region's village: an organic, inter-connected whole that centres round the bar and restaurant. Rooms have been conceived as comfortable living spaces as well as an ethnographical testament to all that is local. And the restaurant's menu, as you'd expect, offers the same time-tried recipes that you might find in any traditional Alpujarran home. Mariano has recently created a bodega with a remarkable series of hand-painted ceramic tiles inspired by grapes, wine and the harvest: be sure to take time to visit it if you stay. And check with Mariano for details of the courses and walking excursions that are organised at La Alquería.

To see & do nearby: Walking and riding, visit to the farm's bodega and olive press, and visits to the villages of the Alpujarra.

CASA RURAL LAS CHIMENEAS

Calle Amargura 6, 18493 Mairena

Tel: 958 760 352 or 629 017 481 Fax: 958 760 004
Email: info@alpujarra-tours.com
www.alpujarra-tours.com

Management:	Emma & David Illsley
Closed:	Never
Bedrooms:	2 Doubles and 1 Twin in main house, 2 Studio/Apartments and 1 House with 2 Doubles
Prices:	Double/Twin/Apartment €70 including VAT
Meals:	Breakfast included (athough not for apartment), Packed Lunch €5, Dinner €20 excluding wine.

Directions: From Granada A92 east towards Almería. After passing Guadix take the exit 312 for La Calahorra then go over pass of 'El Puerto de la Ragua' to Laroles. Here right to Mairena. Take the second right into the village and park in the square. Las Chimeneas is just 30 metres off south-east corner of square.

David and Emma lived and worked in many different parts of Europe before heading for La Alpujarra, inspired in part by English author Gerald Brenan's writings about the area. They arrived in the right place at just the right time. An architect who had completely restored this old village house had decided to move on. It's easy to see why they fell in love with the house and the village which has only recently been discovered by the expats in search of their *Shangri-La*. It's a quiet, friendly place where you're as likely to see passing mules as you are cars. The village looks out across a deep *barranco* to the distant Contraviesa mountains. The atmosphere that the whole house seems to breathe is one of wholesome, uncluttered simplicity. There's a high-ceilinged guest lounge/diner with a hearth, books, rocking chairs and light streaming in from its south-facing windows. The bedrooms are every bit as attractive and most are large, some have terraces and all have wonderful old floors and antique furniture. Many of the guests at Las Chimeneas come to explore the mountains surrounding the village and the Illsleys know all of its loveliest pathways.

To see & do nearby: Walking (high peaks of 8000 feet easily accessible), horse-riding, visits to other little-known villages such as Júbar.

HOTELS 122 – 125

JAÉN

LA CASONA DEL ARCO

Calle Sacramento 3, 23440 Baeza

Tel: 953 747 208 Fax: 953 747 209
Email: hotel@lacasonadelarco.com
www.lacasonadelarco.com

Management:	Ramón Mola
Closed:	Never
Bedrooms:	14 Standard and Superior Twin/Doubles and 4 Junior Suites
Prices:	Double/Twin €75-107, Superior Double €96-128, Junior Suite €112-139 incl. VAT
Meals:	Breakfast included, snacks available in cafeteria throughout the day.

Directions: From Granada A44/E902 towards Madrid. Just past Jaén on A316 for Úbeda. Take first exit for Baeza and follow signs for 'centro urbano' to the Plaza de España. Here right up Calle Barreras to the Puerta de Úbeda. Hotel is just through arch on left where you can normally find parking.

Recently awarded the accolade *Unesco World Heritage* site Baeza is amongst Andalucía's loveliest towns yet remains way off the tourist-beaten trail. It's been saved, perhaps, by being a two hour drive from Granada and on the way to ... well, nowhere really. Within the confines of its historic centre are numerous Renaissance palaces and churches and a number of boutique hotels. My favourite is La Casona del Arco. The hotel is just yards from the Puerta de Úbeda, a ten minute stroll from the bars and restaurants of the Paseo de la Constitución and the same distance from Baeza's wonderful cathedral. The elegant façade of dressed stone gives a first visual taste of La Casona yet belies the size of the hotel: beyond the fine wrought iron door are eighteen bedrooms and suites, a walled garden with swimming pool, an airy breakfast room-cum-cafeteria as well as a spa with sauna, jacuzzi and massage room. Of the bedrooms I particularly liked the attic ones with their parquet floors and sloping ceilings but all are as smart as smart can be with subtle lighting, colour-matched fabrics, antique and reproduction furniture and first class bathrooms. La Casona and Baeza more than justify that detour through the olive groves of Machado's poems: this is a hotel with a big heart and great value, too.

To see & do nearby: Úbeda and Baeza, the Cazorla Park, day trips to Jaén and Granada, visits to local olive mills.

PALACIO DE LA RAMBLA

Plaza del Marqués 1, 23400 Úbeda

Tel: 953 750 196 Fax: 953 750 267

Email: hotel@palaciodelarambla.com

www.palaciodelarambla.com

Management:	Elena Meneses de Orozco
Closed:	Mid July – early August
Bedrooms:	2 Doubles, 4 Twins and 2 Suites
Prices:	Double/Twin €115, Suite €125 + 7% VAT
Meals:	Breakfast included, no other meals. Several bars and restaurants on your doorstep.

Directions: From Granada A44/E902 towards Madrid then A316 to Úbeda. Follow signs 'centro ciudad' then at second of Hospital de Santiago's two towers turn right. Take second turning to left and continue to end of street to Palacio de la Rambla which you'll see to the left: normally you can find parking by turning right.

Úbeda's old town bears witness to a period when a flourishing woolen trade made many a fortune for its merchant class. With their new-found riches they commissioned a series of exquisite Renaissance mansions and churches whose opulence takes you by surprise. But nowadays the place is a sleepy market town and well off the tourist-beaten trail. The brightest star amongst its 'golden age' architects was Andrés de Vandelvira and it was he who was entrusted with the building of La Rambla. He designed a mansion house of delicate proportions, wrapped around a cloistered and galleried patio: every inch the noble residence. The Meneses de Orozco family have decorated the palace in keeping with its blue-blooded past: masses of the family's finest antiques, oil paintings of their forebears, rich fabrics, French chandeliers, engravings from England. It's easy to see why King Alfonso XIII should have chosen to stay here when he passed through the town on a royal tour of duty. Bedrooms are airy and high-ceilinged, bathrooms superb and the breakfast much better than most. Add to this the quiet, out-of-time atmosphere of the place, the ever-smiling manager Rosa, beautiful old Úbeda right on your doorstep and you begin to get the measure of this exceptional hostelry.

To see & do nearby: Walking in the Cazorla Park, the old towns of Úbeda and Baeza, day trips to Córdoba, Jaén and Granada.

HOTEL LA FINCA MERCEDES

Ctra de la Sierra km 1, 23476 La Iruela

Tel: 953 721 087 Fax: 953 720 624

Email: info@lafincamercedes.com

www.lafincamercedes.com

Management:	Mercedes Castillo
Closed:	Never
Bedrooms:	9 Twin/Doubles and 1 Triple
Prices:	Double/Twin €39-42, Triple €48-52 + 7% VAT
Meals:	Breakfast €5, Lunch/Dinner €13 excluding wine

Directions: From Úbeda take the N322 towards Albacete then A315 and A319 to Cazorla. Here continue up to large square at centre of town and turn left at signs for La Iruela. Stay on this road, pass just beneath La Iruela, and La Finca Mercedes is on the left after 1 km.

Jaén Province · Map 8 · HOTEL 124

If you're looking for a cheap and cheerful place to lay your head when visiting the wonderful Cazorla Park you couldn't do better than book a night or two at this modest hotel. The life and soul of the place is Mercedes Castillo and it's fitting that the hotel was named after her. I stayed for several nights when researching a walking guide and was made to feel a part of the family. Things here are on a human scale. The bedrooms are of average size, decorated with simple pine furniture and the best look out across the vast expanse of olive groves that lies to the east of Cazorla. They are quiet, comfortable and warm in the winter months: temperatures can plummet in this part of Andalucía. The dining room has the same inviting, snug feel about it with an open hearth, low beamed ceiling and paintings of Cazorla and the sea interspersed with a collection of hunting trophies. Simple, regional dishes are on the menu, some of the veggies are home grown. Mercedes' two daughters, rather quieter than Mum, are often there to serve you and always invite you to a chupito at the end of the meal. The family also own a small farm with a pool, Cortijo Belfalá, which can be rented on a daily or weekly basis. *Details on request.*

To see & do nearby: The Cazorla Natural Park, the old towns of Cazorla, Úbeda and Baeza and their Renaissance architecture.

MOLINO LA FARRAGA

Calle Camino de la Hoz s/n, Apartado de Correos 1, 23470 Cazorla

Tel: 953 721 249 Fax: 953 721 249

Email: reservas@molinolafarraga.com

www.molinolafarraga.com

Management:	Marisa Muñoz
Closed:	December 10 – February 25
Bedrooms:	1 Single, 3 Doubles, 3 Twins and 1 Suite
Prices:	Single €50, Double/Twin €70, Suite €100 + 7% VAT
Meals:	Breakfast included

Directions: In Cazorla follow signs for 'Ruinas de Santa María': very narrow streets! At far side of the Plaza de Santa María take road leading between ruined church and 'Cueva' restaurant, signposted 'Castillo'. Park on left by sign for La Farraga then cross bridge and continue on foot for 100 metres to La Farraga.

You reach Cazorla by way of a vast sea of olive groves. After this seemingly endless monoculture, it comes as a relief to see a rugged mountain crest rising up in the distance. And standing sentinel to the sierra you catch sight of Cazorla, a white town clinging to its steep eastern flank. The prettiest part of the town is a delightful small square by the ruined church of Santa María and just up the valley from here the old mill house of La Farraga must surely be one of the very nicest places to stay in Andalucía. You abandon your car 100 yards before La Farraga, cross a small bridge and then follow a riverside path to the mill. Its wonderfully verdant garden is crisscrossed by water channels, birds sing amongst the foliage, and your gaze is drawn upwards to the majestic crags of the Cazorla mountains. Inside the mill house the feel is one of simple, solid comfort and well-being. Rooms vary in dimensions, all are beautifully decorated and feel airy and peaceful. This could be a fabulous base for a walking holiday: a gorgeous circular trail leads straight out from the house and, for the more adventurous, there are more challenging walks which are as beautiful as any in Andalucía: see my guide *Walking In Andalucía*.

To see & do nearby: The Cazorla Natural Park, the old towns of Cazorla, Úbeda and Baeza and their Renaissance architecture.

HOTELS 126 – 129